REAL
CONNECTIONS

Ministries to Strengthen Church and Community Relationships

Joy Skjegstad
Heidi Unruh

JUDSON PRESS
PUBLISHERS SINCE 1824

VALLEY FORGE, PA

Interior design by Hampton Design Group.
Cover design by Megan Sizemore.

Library of Congress Cataloging-in-Publication data
Library of Congress Control Number: 2021934885

Printed in the U.S.A.
First printing, 2021.

Joy:
To my husband Bradley Schrag,
for being with me on all of my adventures,
offering encouraging words and
excellent food all the way.

Heidi:
To my husband Jim,
for showing me each day
the value of living connected.

And to my mentor and friend Ron Sider—
"I thank my God every time
I think of you" (Philippians 1:3).

CONTENTS

Acknowledgments

JOY:

It was a lucky day when I got to work with Heidi Unruh on a project some years ago—when we got together we "stuck," and have been friends and colleagues ever since. She is tireless in seeking to do good, vastly creative and an incredible editor and writer. Thank you, Heidi, for everything you did to make this book happen.

I am grateful for the churches where I have served on the staff and as a consultant, places where I learned so much about effective ministry, building strong relationships, and letting the Holy Spirit work: Park Avenue United Methodist Church and Sanctuary Covenant Church and consulting clients Greater Friendship Missionary Baptist Church, Spirit of the Lord Church, Normandale Lutheran Church, Hennepin Avenue United Methodist, and Redeemer Lutheran in North Minneapolis come to mind immediately when I think of places of deep learning for me.

And a thank you to my own church, Messiah Episcopal, where I have been given the opportunity to try a number of visioning and listening processes over the years. Teaching for Central Baptist Theological Seminary, and teaching and coaching for the Indiana Center for Congregations and several United Methodist conferences around the country, have also taught me a great deal about the church and its potential.

And to my circle of closest friends who are my own real connections every day. They pray for me, advise me, love me, and go on shopping and art appreciation excursions with me: Paul and Libby, Jessica and Jordan, Amy and Dave, B.J., Pat, Nora, Vanessa, Linda, Denise, Mary Lou, Dave and Diane, and members of our small group.

My children, Ethan and Julia, inspire me to do my work every day and are a source of ideas in how to keep talking even when you don't always agree. And to Brad, your love lifts me up.

Acknowledgments

HEIDI:

My family supported this project, embracing the irony of my spending long hours away from the people to whom I am most deeply connected to write about connections. Jim, Maurice, Jacob, Elise, Yu'Nique—my bond with you is a gift I treasure. Jim, thank you for your feedback on the manuscript, and many years of conversations leading up to it.

Thank you to First Mennonite Church and pastor Tonya Wenger for your prayers and encouragement through this difficult season. "May the Lord make your love increase and overflow for each other and for everyone else" (1 Thessalonians 3:12, NIV).

I am blessed to be part of an amazing network of church and nonprofit leaders dedicated to the well-being of our community of Reno County, Kansas. This group practices what Joy and I preach about cultivating real connections in the pursuit of shared vision. Numerous individuals in my community read chapters and offered feedback, shared their experiences and insights, and cheered me on—as well as inspiring me by their example: Annette, Beth, Bob, Bobbie, Carolyn, David, Denice, Jane, Jeanne, Jim, John, Kari, Laurie, Marietta, Megan, Nancy, Rachel, Rebecca, Sarah, Seth, Shawna, Star. Thank you!

Appreciation also to Hutchinson Community Foundation for convening dialogues and leading a relational approach to community change that helped shape my perspective on connections. My work also benefited from supportive coaching by colleagues at the Kansas Leadership Center.

A special note of gratitude to my colleague Dr. Tom Lutz for generously allowing me to delay our project (Equipping Christians for Kingdom Purpose in Their Work) so that I could pursue this timely interlude.

If you ever get to write a book while the world is going bonkers, I recommend having Joy Skjegstad for a partner. In fact I recommend Joy for just about everything. She is brilliant, creative, perceptive, compassionate, and one of the best people I know for getting down to what matters. I have never laughed so much, or felt so cared for, during a writing project. Here's to our ongoing connection.

JOINT:

This book project was launched in the thick of a pandemic, racial reckoning, and political unrest. As Joy and I talked with pastors and ministry leaders, we heard the heart cry of so many struggling to follow the light of Jesus and lead well through this dark time. We appreciate you.

Over the years we have worked with many congregations, pastors, and denominational leaders who have inspired us with their example of faithful, creative ministry. Together we say thank you to the churches that allowed us to share their stories, and to the church leaders who allowed us to quote you. We especially acknowledge the Center for Congregations and their support for our work with congregations in Indiana, including the ones mentioned in the book: Bethel Community Church, Broadway United Methodist Church, Central Christian Church Disciples of Christ, Christ the King Lutheran Church, First Christian Church, Indy Metro Church, Mount Pleasant United Methodist Church, St. John Lutheran Church, Trinity Church of Indianapolis, and Trinity Missionary Baptist Church. If we had more pages in the book, this list would be longer.

We also thank our colleagues around the country who read excerpts, offered feedback, connected us with resources, and shared quotes with us.

We are grateful to Judson Press and editor Dr. Cheryl Price for accepting this project. Both of us have published previously with Judson Press and feel we have a special connection with this team.

Introduction
What a Pandemic Taught Us about Relationships While Keeping Us Apart

In March 2020, when the country shut down, the two of us (Joy and Heidi) had to cancel plans, like so many others. Ironically, Joy was supposed to travel to work with a big room of church leaders on laying out "the future of the church," and Heidi was supposed to be giving a workshop at a church on "how to build connections in your community"!

Instead, new ministry conversations developed. We reflected on how the pandemic and social unrest were affecting congregations, including our own. We talked with church leaders about the new challenges of maintaining connections in the congregation and being a positive presence in their communities. We researched how churches around the nation were responding to the waves of crisis, and we witnessed the extraordinary compassion, creativity, and perseverance of God's people.

We began sharing some of these principles and practices with churches (virtually). Every time we presented, we were reminded of both the depth of the struggle and the vital presence of the Spirit in the body of Christ.

One theme that emerged in these conversations is how the church has been wrestling with tough questions about its purpose. What we heard over and over again was the critical role of churches in helping people develop connections with each other. We thought we would share how each of us personally processed our church experiences.

Joy: What Is the Church Even For?

I've been attending church at least once a week since I was just a few days old. It's a practice imbedded in my life. During the pandemic, I realized that I hadn't asked many questions about the church's purpose. When our services moved online, I found myself wondering, How do we be the church when we aren't gathering together in person? Where is the church if we are not meeting in our buildings? Is there church when we can't sing together or shout out to God in one voice?

I kept returning to this question: If church is something we watch on television, do we need to be together in one place, in person, to experience it? Many of us realized that we could stay in the comfort of our own homes and experience a worship service while wearing pajamas, petting the cat, lying on the floor with the guinea pigs (me), or eating a cup of yogurt (also me).

But something was missing. Some expressed the view that the virtual church was here to stay, but this did not feel like church to me. It became clear that this was because of the lack of connection with people. I realized that church is less about programs and worship services, and much more about the community I had formed with my fellow parishioners.

I stayed in touch with my closest friends from church during lockdowns, but it was other people in the congregation that I missed the most—being able to kneel down next to Janet's walker and say something encouraging to her; to comment on the progress of all the babies and their cuteness (so many babies!); to approach someone I don't know well and say that I appreciated their presentation in Sunday school; to sing across the aisle from our Karen parishioners (immigrants from Myanmar), who were singing the same song in their language while the rest of us sang in English. There is a dissonance to that, but it is also strangely beautiful—it seems right when you hear it.

Being at church was always this whirl of encouraging one another, sharing ideas, telling jokes, getting to know someone better, chatting about ministry challenges and opportunities. Without really realizing it, I had formed this web of connections around me. It's what I missed the most when we weren't gathering in person.

Heidi: What Does Normal Mean, Anyway?

When the shutdowns began, my church—like churches everywhere—had to make rapid, radical adjustments to this crazy new reality. It was disorienting. I saw the burden that church leaders carried, trying to hold the church together. I felt the kindness of our church's members as they reached out to one another, making sure everyone was OK.

As the pandemic dragged on, I sensed a growing weariness, anxiety, and restlessness. Churches faced layers of crises: finances, physical and mental health, stresses on family life, the grief of losses, confronting racial injustices, political strife. It was impossible to predict tomorrow's news, let alone the big question: When could church life get back to normal?

I began to wonder what "normal" meant, and whether we could get back to it—or whether that should even be the goal.

The reality, perhaps, is that change and uncertainty are always just around the corner. But in "normal" times, some of us are privileged to maintain the illusion that life is static. The pandemic exposed hidden areas of pain in our social relationships, alarming levels of isolation, and a lack of authentic, caring community. I thought about a question posed by Rev. Leroy Barber: "Why would we want to go back to normal?"

In this stress to our systems, could we find the gift of openness to new ways of doing church, of being church?

For example, we might shift from "going to church" to "gathering as the church." We might refocus on church as a community of people in relationship with God and one another. Just as we maintain church buildings, we might recognize that congregational connections also need regular tending with skill and care.

In my church, the bright spots have been all about relationships: Reconnecting with attenders who moved away but found our online services. Youth and seniors stepping up to stay connected. Strengthened collaboration with other churches and nonprofits to meet community needs. An energized Zoom group working toward racial reconciliation. Celebrating every precious in-person meeting—even just running into another church member at the store.

We can cope better with inevitable uncertainty if we know how to cultivate enduring relationships. When "new" is normal, we must rely more on one another for support, to adapt together to whatever comes next.

Looking Toward Our Future

We wanted to write this book because 2020, that year like no other, convinced us that healthy connections need to be more at the center of church life. We don't want to go back to a disconnected way of being church. We share the optimism of the former Surgeon General, Vivek Murthy, who commented, "If we recommit to people and to social relationships, we have the opportunity to use this moment to recenter our lives on people. If we do that, I believe we can come out of this pandemic more connected, more fulfilled and resilient than when the pandemic began."[1]

Our experiences, as well as many conversations with church leaders, have taught us four key points.

Listening to each other is more important than ever. If we assumed we understood what other people needed during this time of incredible upheaval and devastation, we soon discovered we were mistaken. We think it's time to listen to each other, among church members and in the community. We challenge you to build real listening into the way you do every ministry.

Knowing your neighbors is more important than ever. Hyper-local approaches to helping people meet needs and stay connected are effective, and sometimes they are the only option. Knowing the people in your neighborhood provides hope, encouragement, and practical kinds of help in tough times.

Having connections in the community is more important than ever. Churches that were already connected to community partners like schools, hospitals, and senior living complexes were in the best position to offer help during the pandemic. They had already built trust with partners, so they were able to swing quickly into action.

Being able to have difficult conversations is more important than ever. This time of deep division made it glaringly apparent that Christians need to be able to have conversations about difficult issues, even if that is risky or feels uncomfortable. We can't mirror the culture on this one. We need to find ways to model loving, honest dialogue that engages people as individuals, not labels.

The Church Is Not Closed

When the pandemic stripped churches of the ability to use their buildings, gather on Sunday mornings, or operate their usual programs, questions about the church's core nature and purpose took center stage. As we talked with churches in this context of uncertainty and chaotic change, this affirmation stood out:

> The church is not closed.
> Our mission is not on hold.
> Our calling to love our neighbors has not changed.
> How we do it is evolving.

Over and over again, what rose to the top for this evolving question of how we do church is the need for real connections between people, both within the congregation and in the community, and the church's role in helping those connections develop.

Note

1. Interview with Rachel Martin for NPR *Morning Edition* (May 11, 2020); see also Vivek Murthy, *Together: The Healing Power of Human Connection in a Sometimes Lonely World* (New York: Harper Wave, 2020).

1
Real Connections
Relationships Make All the Difference

Why a Book about Connections?

There are seasons when the church is challenged more than ever to become relevant to a changing landscape and step forward into new ways of being the church. The year 2020 was like that. Through the waves of crisis, one thing that stands out is our elemental hunger and thirst for real relationships. In this yearning we see both the potential, and the struggles, of being the body of Christ.

Churches could play a major role in addressing what has been called an "epidemic of social isolation." But for too many people, *church is a lonely place* that lacks a warm welcome and opportunities to build real connections. Church can be an isolating experience if people don't really talk to you, you are outside the circle, and there is no welcoming invitation to plug in.

Churches could strengthen communities by developing strong relational connections in their neighborhood. But churches often *miss out on getting to know the people in their community*. Well-intentioned community ministry programs often focus exclusively on meeting material needs or attracting new members rather than forming personal relationships. And church members often don't personally get to know the people in the neighborhoods where they live.

Churches could equip members to cultivate relationships with people who are different from them. Because of our oneness in Christ, church could be a place where we spend time with people who look and act differently from us, where our biases are challenged, where we learn to have hard conversations, and where we are sent out to build caring connections and work together for justice with those who struggle. But too often, congregational life *reinforces our sameness and insulates us from difference.*

What may be emerging out of this crisis is a reenergized vision for what the body of Christ can become:

• a hub of mutual care where people can minister to one another well during times of sickness and grief

• a fellowship where socially isolated individuals can find friends

• a bridge during a time of racial reckoning and political division, bringing diverse people together for honest conversation

• a catalyst of community relationships, reaching out to listen and collaborate so that more people can share in real connections through the love of Christ.

One of the reasons why churches do not live up to this vision is that the structure and culture of church life can work against real connections. It's easy to fall into the trap of measuring church success by "bodies, bucks, and bricks." Having lots of people in a big church building or supporting a generous budget is not necessarily an indicator of the quality of relationships within and beyond the congregation.

Church leaders may also feel pressure to maintain lots of programs—men's and women's groups, Bible studies, volunteer service, VBS—that keep people engaged in church life. But too much routine activity can contribute to a busyness that impedes authentic connections with one another. We need to develop new skills, strategies, and priorities for

A Crisis of Connection in the United States

• 40 percent of adults in America report regularly feeling lonely.

• One in four people say they have no one they can talk to about a personal problem.

• Young adults who heavily use social media are three times more likely to feel socially isolated.

• A quarter of all households are someone living alone (among seniors, a third live alone).[1]

2

the body of Christ to move toward its potential for meaningful relationships, in this season of crisis and beyond.

Moving Relationships to the Driver's Seat

We believe a primary purpose of the church is to facilitate relationships that lead to a closer walk with God and a more Christ-like concern for others. The more that congregations invest in relationships, the more we realize the full meaning of the gospel for ourselves, and the more meaningfully we can share it with others. We hope to engage more Christians in seeking deeper, more diverse connections, as an integral part of our spiritual life and a central part of God's plan for the body of Christ.

In other words, we want to see relationships moved into the front seat of church life. Real connections should be at the forefront of everything we do in the church—whether these efforts are focused on the church's members or in the broader community. Connections should drive programs and activities, not the other way around. If connections are lost, then programs serve little purpose.

When churches shift the focus to relationships, they start measuring different things: whether people feel welcomed and included, whether people are making friends at church, whether community ministries are built on listening and collaboration, whether Christians are confronting hard issues in a way that fosters greater unity, to name a few examples. To make progress toward these relational outcomes, congregations need to be intentional about developing settings, activities, and conversations where real connections can be made. This book provides examples and ideas for this work.

We want to say from the outset that we are not trying to change Western church's mission statement, vision, or style of worship. We believe that the goal of living more connected lives is consistent with many different expressions of the body of Christ.

We recognize the challenge of emphasizing connections in the face of a culture that values surface interactions over authenticity, focuses (sometimes aggressively) on what divides people, rewards busyness, and idealizes living independently from others. Resisting these cultural norms in order to foster real connections takes time, effort, and leadership. It isn't easy—but it doesn't have to be too complicated. We hope this book helps you feel inspired and encouraged to take a few next steps forward.

What Do Real Connections Look Like?

We say "connection" to cover a range of ways that people build meaningful, personal ties with one another. A real connection goes beyond exchanging pleasantries. Just sitting side by side on a church pew, or living next door, or working together on a project does not necessarily lead to getting to know one another.

In this book, connections are always personal in a way that gets beyond surface level interactions. They involve an element of self-disclosure, as well as curiosity about the other person's life. Connecting also requires intentional effort to get to know someone. There are accidental meetings, but not accidental connections. Connections are *real* in the sense of authenticity. A real connection—"getting real" with someone—entails some degree of vulnerability and unpredictability, and thus an element of risk.

Building Real Connections Is Not the Same As …

Serving people. Assisting people with meeting basic needs is an essential part of what it means to be a Christian, but helping people is not the same as having a relationship with them.

Being friendly. Being cordial and nice to people is an important first step in building a connection, but isn't sufficient. There are many friendly churches where you can attend without making a real friend.

Friendship evangelism. While the good news of Christ can spread through relationships, our focus includes building connections both within and outside the church.

Church growth. Being more authentically relational may well improve chances of drawing people to your church and keeping them there. However, we discourage viewing relationships as a means to an end—i.e., build connections in order to increase attendance. We believe relationships have value in and of themselves.

Finally, our definition of connection also involves caring. When you are connected with someone, you take an interest in what happens to them. Note that you can care about someone without their being your favorite person to hang out with. A connection does not always grow into a friendship, but it implies the possibility that might happen.

Connections fall along a continuum of intensity and openness. Relationships[2] typically develop in stages, which we've nicknamed *coffee house*, *living room*, *laundry room*, and *emergency room*.

Coffee house. The first stage of connection means taking a step to get to know someone better: "Let's grab some coffee and talk!" A coffee house connection can also represent a relationship of checking in with someone from time to time, like a neighbor you talk with over the fence, or an elderly church member you visit once a month. There is mutual sharing, if not much intimacy. This level of connection also includes seeking out diverse perspectives in listening projects.

Living room. This type of connection involves personal interaction that moves from acquaintance to friend. There is a more personal and open quality to the relationship, and enough trust that you would invite the person into your home. Examples of living room connections include a church friend that you look forward to hanging out with after the service, or a youth you are mentoring, or a work colleague you meet weekly for prayer. Living room connections enrich our lives.

Laundry room. Many of us spruce up the living room for company . . . but the laundry room remains a mess. This stage means openness to the messy parts of relationship. We let people see us as we are, not just as we want to be seen. With authenticity and vulnerability comes the risk of conflict, disappointment, and hurt—but also a deeper appreciation for one another, and mutual influence. Laundry rooms are not only where messes are shared but also where restoration can happen, and deeper unity can be forged.

Emergency room. The deepest connections mean being part of someone's support system. Literally, these are the people you would rely on to take you to the ER. A third of adults (half of adults living in poverty) say that in an emergency or hardship, they have no one outside of family they could call on for help.[3] We all need a few people we trust to be there for us, no matter what. These are deeply rewarding friendships (some use the term "chosen family") that share the highs as well as lows in life.

We lift up the hope that Christians broaden their circle of connections to get to know people different from themselves; that they might lean on God as they take risks to deepen their bonds of friendship; that everyone might know that even at their messiest there is someone who cares about them; and that no one should have to face life's hardest moments alone.

Real Connections in Theological Perspective

Why is building connections a central part of God's plan for the body of Christ? Because we are created for relationship! From first to last, God's loving plan for humankind flows through relationships.[5]

We have a relational origin story. Humankind was created in the image of God, designed to walk with our Creator and to partner with one another in close connection. It is not good for humans to be always alone (Genesis 2:18).

Joy's Connection Story

A few years back, God began doing a new work in me, and part of that involved sending me a mentor. She said we were going to do life together as friends, and we did just that. She invested in me regularly, listening, providing advice and honest feedback, spending time with my family, being there for special events. I felt that her interest in and commitment to me reflected God's love for me, so I began experiencing faith in a new way.

Her direct way of talking to me about my spiritual life (and the rest of my life) caused me to consider my motivations for why I was putting so much energy into certain things. This relationship was one of a kind for me (so far). I can look back and see the ways that I turned toward a focus on service, a deeper connection to family and friends, and a renewed sense of calling, because of the time she spent with me. She went to be with God in heaven a few years back. I miss her so, but the impact of this relationship on my life continues.

Heidi's Connection Story

I can't remember how D.[4] and I started being friends at church—perhaps chatting after the service, or at a fellowship meal. D. impressed me with her beautiful smile, graceful bearing, and courage in coping with one hardship after another. Her faith saw her through a traumatic childhood, an abusive marriage, and the grinding stress of poverty and racism. I appreciated the trust she placed in me, despite hurtful encounters she'd had with other white women. She shared her struggles with me but always asked how I was doing too. When her son made progress at school, I cheered. When I finally became pregnant, she cheered.

I told her about my desire for a more regular prayer life. She proposed we call one another first thing in the morning, before waking kids up for school. So once a week, my phone would ring before dawn, and we would groggily share our updates on life, pray for one another, then recite a Scripture passage we had decided to memorize together. This tradition of weekly calls continued for months, even after I moved to another state. It helped me feel connected with the church family I had left behind. Eventually, we drifted apart, but the memory of our friendship remains a cherished gift.

We have brokenness in our relationships. In Genesis, the first humans dragged one another down as they rejected God, leading to great suffering. Pride, selfishness, and hard-heartedness get in the way of life-giving relationships.

We are redeemed through relationship. Our salvation comes through Immanuel, "God with us" (Matthew 1:23). After his resurrection, Jesus joyfully reunited with his circle of connections, then sent them out to connect with new people.

We are redeemed for relationship. Much of the New Testament deals with how people who love Jesus should treat one another. Investing in relationship is an essential aspect of mission: "So deeply do we care for you that we are determined to share with you not only the gospel of God but also our own selves" (1 Thessalonians 2:8).

Our faith grows through relationships. Engaging with others shows us where we are most in need of transformation and pushes us to rely on

God. The early church valued connectedness as a core part of its spiritual life, as illustrated in Acts 2:42: "They devoted themselves to the apostles' teaching and fellowship, to the breaking of bread and the prayers."

Our destiny is to live in redeemed relationships. The book of Revelation describes God's ultimate plans for humanity using the most intimate of relational imagery, a wedding. People from all nations and cultures will bring their diverse gifts together into the city where God lives among the people. The redeemed will experience relationships as God intended— with no tears and no goodbyes.

Because God has wired us for relationship, it is not surprising that as individuals, as churches, and as a community, we need connectedness to thrive—even to survive. This theological truth has been reaffirmed by so- ciology, psychology, neuroscience, and even physics, all giving us a clearer picture of how relationships are essential.[6]

Benefits of Focusing on Relationships

Here are a few of the many ways that real connections, especially deeper relationships, advance the work of the church.

Church vitality. Connectedness may not be a surefire path to numerical growth—but church growth is difficult without it. A well-connected church is more visible in the community, more attractive to unchurched folks, more likely to rally broad engagement, and better able to "close the back door," as they say about the tendency for people to slip out of church life unnoticed. New relationships bring new energy.[7]

Congregational care. If we don't know the person beside us in the pew, we might never learn that they have just had a family member arrested or received devastating health news. If we are intentional about having relationships with each other, we are better able to min- ister to each other as needed. (Chapter 8 offers suggestions for con- necting with someone going through a difficult time.) If parishioners don't tend to one another, they may lean more on church staff, which contributes to burnout.

I (Joy) have had people pull me aside at times at church and say things like, "You look sad or stressed. Can I pray for you?" This was so meaningful to me! They were able to do this because we interact regularly.

Revitalized community ministry. A church that makes relational connections in the community and listens well is better positioned to respond to issues in effective ways. It takes personal investment to discover who lives in the community, what they are facing, what assets and gifts are in the neighborhood, and how to collaborate well with local groups.

Authentic witness. Younger generations especially may be tuned out to a message of faith that is shared in words alone, or that comes in flashy packaging. They need to see it lived out in the context of meaningful relationships, unafraid of the hard places or the hard conversations.

Effective advocacy. Churches can play a role in building connections around common goals. The more that people know and trust one another, the better a community can rally to make progress on big challenges like housing or employment. "The connections among local people are what awaken the power of families and neighborhoods to weave the social fabric of an abundant community."[8]

In sum, building connections is at the heart of all that God calls the church to do and to be.

Exploring the State of Connections in Church Life

By stripping away other features of church life, the 2020 pandemic exposed the raw wiring of our connections. Taking an honest look at the relational aspects of your church's ministry will help you see where the gaps are in helping people build connections and could suggest changes in the way you do things. (See the relational assessment in the online resources.)

We understand that focusing on connections is hard (and especially daunting for introverts!). This type of work is imprecise and even countercultural. We could share many stories with you about the ways we personally haven't lived up to this vision, so you'd know we don't see ourselves as gurus in this field but passionate fellow learners.

We present some challenging ideas for churches to consider—but it is not our intention to pile on to an already overwhelming situation. Our goal is not to judge, but to nudge. We care about the wellbeing of churches and believe that focusing on relationships offers a restorative path forward.

Each chapter offers suggestions and strategies for growing toward a more connected life. We hope you discover ways that your church—and you personally—may be ripe for growth toward authentic connections.

Take a Step

We want to dispel the notion that every church should excel in every opportunity for building relationships. Rather, we encourage the goal of intentional, prayerful, Spirit-formed progress. What seems like the most fruitful starting place to move toward a more relationship-rich

Real Connections: Book Overview
Chapters 2 and 3 describe essential qualities and skills for building real connections. The next four chapters offer suggestions for how congregations can strengthen the breadth and depth of relationships in specific contexts—within the congregation (chapter 4), in partnership with other churches (chapter 5), with organizations and residents in the community (chapter 6), and in members' neighborhoods (chapter 7).

Chapters 8 and 9 give suggestions for connections in challenging situations: reaching out to people who are struggling or isolated and having hard conversations to bridge deep disagreements. Chapter 10 offers various models for relationally-oriented ministry programs. The final two chapters (11-12) focus on the role of leadership in facilitating connections and managing change as you move relationships to the center of church life.

The appendices include guidelines for staying safe and respecting boundaries in relationships; and sets of questions for conversations that move toward real connections. Additional resources, including guides for congregational and community listening processes and lists of recommended references, are available online at www.judsonpress.com.

way of life? Pick a few ideas and experiment on a small scale to see what works.

Here are just a few examples of practical steps you can take now—in your own life, and in your church—toward building real connections.

Steps that any church member could try:

• The next time you have a conversation with someone, practice listening with your full attention (see chapter 2).

• Introduce yourself to a neighbor you haven't met yet, and start a conversation (chapters 3, 7).

• Set up a coffee time or video chat with someone in the church you haven't seen in a while (chapter 4).

• Call or message someone who has been on the church's prayer list, to say you are thinking of them and ask how they are doing (chapter 8).

• Practice for a hard conversation by asking someone who expresses an opinion: "I'm curious how this came to be important to you? What has influenced your views?" (chapter 9).

Steps that a church leader could try:

• Contact a church that is near yours and introduce yourself; ask if your counterpart is interested in getting together to talk about experiences in ministry in the neighborhood (chapter 5).

• Find out when a neighborhood association meeting or other public event is happening in your church's community and invite another church member or two the church to participate with you; while there, introduce yourself to at least one person (chapter 6).

• Take an inventory of the church's current programs that encourage interaction and relationships (chapter 10).

• Start your next committee meeting by going around the table and asking, "What's on your mind?" (chapter 11).

• Discuss with your church's leadership team why relationships are important and what moving toward a focus on real connections could look like in your congregation (chapter 12).

By their nature, relationships are not grand, sweeping solutions, and they can't be rushed. They unfold slowly through small gestures and long learning curves. But even one new connection can be transformative.

A Message for Pastors
In August 2020, a pastor left a comment on a survey that expressed the way many pastors around the country (probably around the world) have felt through this season of distress:

Feeling disconnected from the people and their needs. Need encouragement, . . . people to come alongside me. But I am tired of virtual everything!!! P.S. MAYBE I JUST NEED A HUG?!!![9]

If you are a pastor, we (Joy and Heidi) affirm our hope that this book should not add to your burden. There is work to be done, but it is everyone's work—not just the pastor's. We hope you can develop supportive relationships, both within and outside the congregation, that help you take care of yourself. You are not alone in the struggle.

If you are a lay person reading this book, as it is appropriate to do so, you might consider offering your pastor a fist bump from time to time—or even a hug.

Notes
1. David Hsu, *Untethered: A Primer on Social Isolation* (2018), www.ReadUntethered.com.
2. The term "relationship" is often associated with family or romantic attachments. We use the word as a synonym for "connection" as defined in this chapter.
3. Barna Research, "Who Are the Lonely in America?" (May 2015), www.barna.com/research/who-are-the-lonely-in-america.
4. The name is withheld for privacy.
5. See John Perkins with Karen Waddles, *He Calls Me Friend: The Healing Power of Friendship in a Lonely World* (Chicago: Moody Publishers, 2019).
6. For more on the vital role of relationships, see the online resource guide for a list of recommended references.
7. See Lee B. Spitzer, *Making Friends, Making Disciples: Growing Your Church Through Authentic Relationships* (Valley Forge, PA: Judson Press, 2010).
8. John McKnight and Peter Block, *The Abundant Community: Wakening the Power of Families and Neighborhoods* (San Francisco: Berrett-Koehler, 2010), 5.
9. "Church Conflict Is a Growing Worry for Pastors during Covid-19," *Banner* (August 21, 2020), https://www.thebanner.org/news/2020/08/lifeway-research-finds-church-conflict-is-a-growing-worry-for-pastors-during-covid-19.

2
Essential Qualities
*Developing Skills and Mindsets for a More
Relational Life*

What does it take to grow toward a more richly connected life?

In this chapter we want to look at a specific set of mindsets, skills, and habits that lead to a life that puts relationships more at the center. These are like the muscles that help you to sustain a posture of openness to new connections and to move toward strengthening relationships. The goal is to equip you to deepen your current relationships and broaden your circle of connections, especially to include people who may be different from you.

The essentials for a relational life that we cover here include listening well; curiosity; mutuality; focusing on assets; availability; and openness. These are themes that will run throughout this book.

Listening Well

Mindful listening meets our deep thirst for connection. The opposite of listening isn't talking, it is indifference. Listening well communicates our respect and care for the other person. Ministry expert David Apple puts it most simply: "Love listens."[1]

Each day offers opportunities to build connections by listening well. Listening could look like inviting a family you just met at church out to lunch, so you can hear more about their story; hosting a focus group at the senior center for ideas on intergenerational ministry; asking your neighbor how they are doing, and giving your full attention to their reply; patiently staying on the phone with a friend as they talk through a challenge they are facing; asking someone you vehemently disagree with to tell you more

Joy's Story: Growing Toward a Relational Life

Since I started intentionally making more room in my life for relationships over a decade ago, I have been learning new things:

To stop talking and start listening. I am a professional talker, and talking is also one of my favorite pastimes—so listening hasn't come naturally to me in life. I can talk continuously (for a long time!) about any topic I am interested in and some that I am not. So, I am learning to make listening my default mode. Listen first, talk later.

To slow life down so I could listen. I've had seasons of life when I ran around all day, and by the time I sat down to dinner with my family I was so exhausted that I couldn't listen to one more thing. I realized that I had no room in life for friends, and I wasn't that great of a family member either. It helped me to rearrange my life to spend less time at work. I understand that not everyone is in a position to do that, but there may be other changes you can make to be more available for listening.

To devote time to connections. Good listening can't be rushed. If there are built-in time constraints on a conversation, such as right before the church service starts, I've learned to ask and make a plan. I have made some good friends over the years by saying, "I am enjoying your story and would love to hear more. I need to go now, but is there another time we could connect?"

about their position; learning more than perhaps you wanted to know about life from the middle school student you tutor.

We talk about listening a lot throughout the book. We give recommendations for creating ministry settings and structures that encourage people to spend time listening to each other. We also offer guidance for a church to develop a listening team to learn more about the church and community (see the guide in the supplemental resources at www.judsonress.com). In addition to being intentional about planning listening activities, we encourage the attitude that hearing what the other person has to say is your highest priority in that moment.

Curiosity

The word "curious" has the same root as the word "care." Being curious is one of the greatest assets in building caring connections.

Being curious means admitting that there are still things that you need to learn from others. This is an important posture as you approach new people, since each one is different from you in some way. So keep your eyes and ears open as you interact with people in your church and your community to discover what you can learn.

Curiosity in action looks like:

• asking questions, then listening to the answers
• being interested in the "why" of people and situations while withholding judgment—What does this person value most? What makes this person so dedicated to their cause?
• learning about what each person brings to the setting they are in, leading to greater appreciation
• being interested in people's life experiences and how that has shaped the congregation or community.

Curiosity leads you to find things you can't readily see or didn't notice before, or what people might not tell you right off. Being curious can help you discover people in your community who were previously invisible to you, perhaps, or an aspect of someone's story that helps you to understand them better.

Curious listening may be especially important, and can lead to meaningful connections, in several contexts.

When your church is planning ministry. Talk with people who have relevant experience, to learn from them. What have they tried that's worked, or not? What is something that only people who have "been there" would know?

When partnering with people or groups who are different from you. When something doesn't fit our expectations, we tend to fill in the gaps with assumptions and stereotypes. One antidote is to be curious, which leads to new understanding and empathy.

When you are tempted to judge. Any time you feel critical, that's a signal to get curious. Remind yourself that you are a learner who doesn't know the whole story. Instead of judging, try to reframe your reaction as a learning opportunity to listen and build compassionate relationship.

When seeking a deeper connection. We can take our familiarity with the people around us for granted. There is always something new to be learned about and from the people we think we know. "Curiosity in almost all relationships (friends, family, neighbors, work) is the beginning of everything truly interesting."[2]

Appendix 2 offers sets of questions that may spark your curiosity and support growing connections in various contexts.

Mutuality

If curiosity is based on the assumption that everyone has something to teach you, mutuality assumes that everyone has something to give. Relationships are a two-way street—I bring something to you, you bring something to me. This sets real connections apart from "helper" relationships in which the benefits flow only one way. In a mutual relationship, each party uses their God-given gifts to bless others, and receives the gifts of others with gratitude. Staying curious and open can draw out what you both bring to the relationship.

Mutuality is closely linked with respect, grounded in the understanding that each individual has been created in the image of God (Genesis 1:27). There can be no real connection without the belief in the equality and dignity of all people. We have to see the person sitting across from us as equally precious, equally gifted, equally valued in God's eyes.

This has been a growth area for me (Heidi). God has had to confront me about the sense of superiority I tend to smuggle into my relationships. A few years ago I had become friends with a woman who wouldn't have checked many of the boxes of what is admired in our culture. I listened to her and treated her kindly, and felt pretty good about myself for that. Then it hit me that if I *really* saw her as an equal, someone just as important and valuable to God as me, I wouldn't pat myself on the back just for being respectful—because everyone deserves respect!

A framework of mutuality encourages us to view relational ministry as an exchange of value, not a one-way sacrifice for others but an investment in others that expects a return. "Mutual respect emerges as congregation and community members learn about one another's talents and dreams. Often, the best assets in mutual ministry are trust, friendship and hope."[3]

A Focus on Assets

The relational quality of mutuality is closely linked with an emphasis on assets—the variety of gifts, experiences, skills, and passions that we can be curious to discover. Each person, each organization, and each community has assets. This focus on assets fits well with biblical ideas of spiritual gifts. Each person is uniquely crafted in the image of God with the gifting to make a difference and bless others: "To each is given the manifestation of the Spirit for the common good" (1 Corinthians 12:7; also Ephesians 2:10; 1 Peter 4:10).

Being focused on assets means delighting in the uniqueness of each person and connecting with them at the point of their giftedness and passions. One person has mechanical skills for fixing things; another is artistic and brings color and new perspectives to every situation. Some people are gifted at nurturing emotional healing. Others have amazing skills for starting businesses or managing projects. Even people's experiences of hardship can become a source of strength. Those who have come through a battle with addictions, for example, often are most effective in reaching out to those still in the midst of the struggle.

A church's community connections are strongest when built on the belief that everyone at the table brings a valuable contribution. We have both worked in communities where residents have been made to feel that they have little to offer—because they lack material wealth, education, or a job with status, for example. Our faith leads us to see how people are gifted even if they have been unable to get ahead in life in the ways that our society typically values. Churches can build on those abilities by helping people discover what they are good at, and then connecting them with others in ways that make life better for everyone.

This mindset of cherishing gifts is abundantly evident at the Church Under the Bridge in Waco, Texas, located in an area where many struggle with homelessness, mental health issues, and addictions. Pastor Jimmy

Dorrell was once showing me (Heidi) around the neighborhood when a man approached, with the appearance of someone whose life had not been easy. Jimmy greeted him by name enthusiastically, and then—to me, unexpectedly—asked him for the news. The man reported the scores of a half-dozen games in several sports. Jimmy thanked him, and he left. Jimmy said, "He's our walking sports page. I can always count on him for my report!"[4] In their Church Under the Bridge community, Jimmy's friend was not defined by his struggles but was known by the gift he loved to share with others.

Moving from Busyness to Availability

Busyness is often perceived as a sign of success and productivity. We have both found that following our own advice about having a relational life has required us to open up our schedules. The "unbusy" life has less packed into it, so it allows more time for relationships.

I (Joy) began taking the entire month of July off from work when my kids were younger, even though it meant completing fewer consulting contracts each year. I ended up being more sane and rested, and my kids got uninterrupted time with me that they needed. Over the years, I have had a number of people ask me what I would do during my month with my kids. I told them that I would sit on my porch watching my kids ride their bikes up and down the sidewalk for a good part of the day.

I made this choice initially to make time for deeper relationships with my children, but creating more space in my life also made room for some deep friendships to develop over the years. Reserving part of almost every Friday for connecting with one other person on a personal basis is another discipline that has led to deep friendships and mentoring relationships.

Some may not be able to have a slower pace because of work schedules or family circumstances. But many of us could consider whether we spend time on non-essentials that could be reallocated to relational engagement. We can also take activities that we normally do alone and be more intentional about doing them with others—like walking the dog, going to the gym, or watching a football game. (We need to affirm, however, that a posture of availability to others does not mean you stop taking time for self-care).

Just as you might look at your financial budget and reduce some expenses in order to donate more, you can look at your time budget to cut back activities in some areas to devote more time to building relationships. Pray over your schedule, and protect time on your calendar for interacting with people. Don't be so focused on the next item on your to-do list that you miss the opportunity for connection right in front of you.

Openness

It's all too easy to remain on the surface of connections: To pass by people on a Sunday morning and call "Hello!" without stopping to converse. Or to say you're fine when you are definitely not. Or to limit your engagement with others on difficult issues to comments on social media, not a real conversation.

What we are proposing in this book is that you have the openness to dig deeper. This means growing more engaged and interested, investing more time, listening more intently, and developing more authenticity in your relationships. Be more intentionally present in your community in a way that allows you to know people and walk together with them.

A hindrance to openness is the ideal of being independent from others—the vision of the rugged individual who can forge their own path, with no help or entanglements. This value is deeply embedded in streams of American culture that view self-sufficiency as the ideal and dependence on others as a sign of weakness. This independence mindset makes it difficult for people to pursue real connections in church and community. It's fine to help others out, strike up a pleasant conversation, ask questions, and listen—but not to ask for help or allow others to generously share their gifts and abilities with us.

Essentially, keeping our struggles hidden from others is linked with lack of trust. Vulnerability and openness require a step—or a leap—of faith.

My (Joy's) family experienced meaningful support from our church friends a few years back, when one of our children made a mistake at school and had to face the harsh consequences. We decided to tell the people around us about it, even though I was afraid how people would react. The most amazing thing to us was that no one judged us. Instead, everyone prayed for us, people checked in with us regularly, and we received a record number of invitations to dinner. We experienced the support we needed, which we wouldn't have received had we kept all of this to ourselves.

Throughout the book, you will see many tips and examples for how to get beyond the surface in church and community relationships. Openness to people translates to risk, uncertainty, lack of control, and change. Going deeper means diving into waters where you can't see the bottom or what lies beneath the surface. This is true for any relationship, but especially in connecting with people seen as "other"—someone we perceive to be different or just difficult.

Making room for the unexpected in our relationships is an act of discipleship. Henri Nouwen notes in his essay, "Moving from Solitude to Community to Ministry," "In the spiritual life, the word discipline means 'the effort to create some space in which God can act.'" Being intentional about your relationships is how you plan a life "in which something can happen that you hadn't planned."[5]

Growing in relationships with others can also deepen and reshape our relationship with God. The essential qualities for building friendships with others can teach us to create space to patiently listen for God's voice; to be humbly curious to learn God's ways; to be mindful of the opportunity in each moment to keep company with God's Spirit. God moves in surprising and powerful ways when we make ourselves open to real connections.

Notes

1. David Apple, *Neighborology: Practicing Compassion as a Way of Life* (Fort Washington, PA: CLC Publications, 2017).

2. Tim Soerens, *Everywhere You Look: Discovering the Church Right Where You Are* (Downer's Grove, IL: InterVarsity Press, 2020), 43–44.

3. Nancy DeMott and Katie Lindberg, "Mutual Ministry," Center for Congregations (January 2018), https://centerforcongregations.org/sites/default/files/Mutual-Ministry-2018.pdf.

4. Jimmy Dorrell shares more stories about this uniquely asset-based, diverse church community (www.churchunderthebridge.org) in *Trolls and Truth: Fourteen Realities about Today's Church That We Don't Want to See* (Birmingham, AL: New Hope Publishers, 2006).

5. Henri Nouwen, "Moving from Solitude to Community to Ministry," *Leadership* (Spring 1995), 81–87.

3
How to Talk with Strangers

*Pointers on Connecting with People You
Don't Know (Yet)*

Why Talk with Strangers?

This book is about building meaningful connections of many kinds. Every meaningful connection starts with a first conversation. Except for your family, every relationship that you have now started out by talking with a stranger. Whether the goal is making your church more welcoming to visitors, getting to know more people in the community, or building a partnership with a church from a different culture, at some point you will probably need to talk with a stranger.

Yet the thought of initiating contact with someone new makes a lot of people quite uncomfortable. Even having a meaningful conversation with someone we might consider a casual acquaintance may be challenging at times. It's easy to get mired in small talk, unable to find a bridge to an authentic connection.

This chapter offers concrete practices for engaging with strangers with genuine interest, thoughtful listening, meaningful conversation, and the possibility of an ongoing relationship.[1] Some of these points may seem basic, but we want everyone to know it's OK to feel like a beginner.

Opening the door to a new connection is a skill that churches can encourage people to develop. Church members will have many opportunities to use this skill. For example, more confidence in talking with strangers may encourage them to:

• reach out to visitors to the church, or people in the congregation they don't know well

• mingle with people from the community at events hosted by the church or community groups

• engage personally with individuals served by the church's community programs

• get to know more of their neighbors and co-workers

• participate in a listening campaign to learn more about the community

• reach out any time they realize someone is lonely and open to making a new friend

Any time you are around someone you haven't gotten to know yet, that is an opportunity to have a connection conversation.

Start with Confidence

The first step to putting others at ease is being comfortable with yourself. You don't have to be the life of the party, the wise mentor, or whatever

Different Gifts for Building Connections
We are all created for relationship, but in different and equally valuable ways. What kind of friend maker are you?

• *Nurturer*—You have a knack for making everyone feel safe and welcome.

• *Sparkler*—You bring positive, fun energy that attracts others.

• *Bridge builder*—You find common ground for building a sense of connectedness.

• *Story catcher*—You build trust to draw out people's life experiences.

• *Practical*—You focus on ways to make people's lives better.

• *Mindful*—You give people deep attention, with empathy and self-awareness.

• *Encourager*—You naturally believe in people and bring out the best in them.

• *Stalwart*—You take your time to get to know people, but then you are staunchly loyal.

• *Other*—What gifts do you offer as a friend?

other ideal you have in mind. Don't try to be whatever you think someone else expects. Be the friend-maker God designed *you* to be. Then you are more likely to accept others for who God designed them to be as well.

Another tip if you get nervous talking with strangers: prepare yourself through self-talk. Being relational requires intentional effort, especially at first. So as you approach a new interaction, warm up like an athlete before a game by reminding yourself of the Five Ps:

- Affirm Purpose *(Building relationships is important, sacred work.)*
- Value Personhood *(This is a unique individual made in God's image and precious in God's eyes.)*
- Keep Perspective *(Feeling awkward for a little while is not so bad.)*
- Stay Positive *(Replace Talking to strangers is scary... with I'm excited to meet someone interesting!)*
- Pray *(May God's Spirit guide me and move through me.)*

Ten Tips on How to Talk to a Stranger

You see someone you've never met before sitting alone at church, or eating alone at the senior center, or walking their dog past your yard. How do you engage?

Following the Spirit's Leading to Connect

I (Joy) typically approach strangers to talk when I feel a nudge from the Holy Spirit. Sometimes this looks like really noticing for the first time someone I walk by regularly at church or in my community. A few times I just became extra curious to learn about some aspect of a stranger's life.

Once, I noticed a young man all alone at the altar after the church service. He had shared about his mother's death in a personal testimony during the service. My husband and I approached him to ask if we could pray for him, and that started a series of conversations that eventually led to a wonderful friendship between our families. This all began with one conversation.

1. *Be welcoming.* This starts with body language. You can send out nonverbal "friend signals" by having an open posture (try not to cross your arms) and establishing eye contact.

As you seek to make a welcoming first impression, also be try to be non-judgmental in your first impression of the other person. Avoid making assumptions based on their appearance. Check your stereotypes—you can't control your first reaction, but you can be intentional about your next response. Think: "This is a person in whom God delights! I wonder what makes this person special?"

2. *Break the ice.* You almost never can go wrong with a simple classic—"Hi, I'm so-and-so. What's your name?" But what to say next? Here are some options. Note that each opener is followed by a question to spark conversation.

• Start with comfortable small talk ("From your cap, it looks like we're both Royals fans. Do you watch a lot of sports?").

• Offer a compliment ("I love your colorful knitted scarf. Did you make that yourself?").

• Make an observation ("I noticed your butterfly tattoo. Does that have special meaning for you?").

• Say something about yourself ("I've lived in this neighborhood since first grade. What's your connection with this neighborhood?").

• Ask for input ("Our church is looking for new ideas about how to connect with youth in the community. So, we have been out talking with high school students. I'd love to hear your thoughts.").

3. *Dive deeper.* There comes a point in most conversations where you can either continue being pleasant but shallow, or take a risk and lean into a deeper connection. Dig a little deeper with someone by asking questions that reflect curiosity with some aspect of their life. This is a valuable conversational skill whether you are just getting to know someone or building on a friendship of many years.[2]

Great starts to curious questions include

- What do you think (or, How do you feel) about . . .
- What was it like to . . .
- What's important to you when it comes to . . .
- What do you find most enjoyable / challenging about . . .
- What are your hopes for . . .

Try framing your questions in a way that invites deeper connection. In addiction to yes/no questions, ask open-ended questions. Instead of asking for more details, ask for stories.

Instead of only . . .	Try going deeper with . . .

Yes/no questions
*Is this your first time visiting
    this church?*
Are you having a good day?
	Open-ended questions
	*What brings you here to
	    church today?*
	*What's been the best part of
	    your day so far?*

Asking for **information**
Where did you go to school?
 	
*How long have you been
    a nurse?*
	Inviting **perspectives** and **stories**
	*What was your favorite class in
	    school?*
	*What made you decide to become
	    a nurse?*

Avoiding **controversial subjects**
*(Not saying anything,
    changing the subject)*
	Exploring **points of view**
	*Who has helped influence
	    your position on X?*
	*What's important to you in
	    your support for X?*

Curious questions get people to talk about what's important to them. They open up space to share stories about the past, insights on the current situation, and dreams for the future. Curious questions make conversations more interesting. (See Appendix 2 for sample curious questions for starting conversations and getting to know people better.)

4. *Ask questions in an invitational way.* Questions are like the oars dipping into unknown waters that keep a conversation gliding forward. Asking questions, like rowing a boat, is a skill that helps determine how far you go. Learn to avoid questions that are intrusive or make people feel they are being interrogated. For example, asking "why" directly can put the listener on the defensive.

Instead of questions that put people on their guard, use questions that invite an engaged reply.

What to Avoid	What to Aim For
Intrusive questions *Where do you live?* *How many kids do* * you have?*	**Interested** questions *How did you come to live* * in this community?* *Are there children in your life?*
Status-revealing questions *Where did you go to college?* *Where do you work?*	**Non-threatening** questions *What do you do for fun?* *What would be your dream job?*
Questions that reflect **bias** *Where are you from?* *Are you married?*	**Inclusive** questions *What were your grandparents like?* *Tell me something about your* * household.*
Questions that make an **assumption** *Isn't this neighborhood great?* *How long have you been* * a Christian?*	Questions that **explore** *How do you feel about this* * neighborhood?* *What is the story of your faith?*
Why questions *Why did you come here today?* *Why aren't you working?*	**Purpose** questions *What brings you here today?* *What are your goals for* * your career?*

If a question or comment slips out that puts the other person on their guard, consider turning the tables by sharing something authentic about yourself.

5. *Listen well.* When you ask a question, stay interested in their answer. Stephen Covey reminds us, "Most of us don't listen with the intent to understand. We listen with the intent to reply."[3] Stay attentive to what the other person is saying in this moment, not what you will say next. "Let everyone be quick to listen, slow to speak" (James 1:19).

The practice of active listening is a vital skill. (See the guide online for recommended resources on active listening). Active listening means giving nonverbal and verbal cues that demonstrate you are fully engaged, including:

- showing you heard what they said ("So, you like this community but wish there were more activities for kids?")
- showing you care ("That sounds like it was a really difficult time for your family.")
- asking for clarification ("What did you mean when you said . . .")
- asking for follow-up ("I'd love to hear more about what that was like for you.")
- affirming their openness ("Thank you for sharing that with me.")

Listening well is linked with being fully present. This is probably the hardest skill in our multi-tasking, device-dependent culture. We've become accustomed to Zoom calls where we only have to make it look on screen like we're paying attention! But being fully present with people is a powerful gift. As essayist David Brooks puts it, "In conversation it's best to act as if attention had an on/off switch with no dimmer. Total focus."[4] When distracting thoughts intrude, remind yourself: What could be more important than this person in front of me?

6. *Listen to the Spirit.* As you listen to the person in front of you, also listen to God's Spirit. Pray for insight on how you can bless this person in the context of your conversation. Don't assume that God has appointed you to solve their problems or confront their life choices. But you may be moved

to offer to pray for concerns they have expressed, to express your caring support, or to ask a follow-up question about their faith story.

7. *Return the serve.* Personal sharing is a critical element that makes the difference between a meaningful conversation and an interview. Don't let your part of the conversation resemble an automatic ball serving machine, lobbing one question after another without offering a personal response. But you should also avoid taking over the conversation by talking too much, like a puppy that gets hold of a ball and decides to chew on it rather than give it back.

Instead, aim for an exciting tennis match where the ball goes back and forth between the players. Even if a question occasionally lands in the net, you can try again and the game goes on.

Each individual has to determine their own comfort level with self-revelation. It's probably unhealthy to discuss a deep trauma with someone you've just met, but you can't expect the other person to shoulder all the vulnerability. The depth of your own sharing will likely set the tone for the conversation, making it safe for the other person to be authentic. As you choose to share from your heart, you give the other person the opportunity to bless you by listening.

Your personal sharing may include your own faith journey as it relates authentically to the conversation at hand. When was a relevant time in your life when God entered into your story?

8. *Stay constructive.* Have you ever had a conversation that turned into a competition for whose life is worse? "You think that's bad? Well, here's the awful thing that happened to me . . ." These types of conversations tend to be real downers.

Of course, there is a valid, necessary place for sharing painful experiences with a caring, attentive listener. But there is a difference between that type of vulnerable sharing that leads to greater trust and healing, and a flat-out gripe fest.

If you sense that the conversation is turning into a zone for complaints, resist the temptation to one-up the negativity; instead, return to a more constructive dialogue. This can happen in several ways. One is to invite the person into deeper sharing that explores insights about their experiences. For example: "Getting criticized by your boss for something you didn't do sounds very frustrating. How do you handle frustrations like that? What do you wish your boss understood about you?"

Another strategy is to redirect the conversation onto a more positive path. For example: "Who has been your favorite boss, and what did you like about them? If you ran a company, how would you treat your employees?"

You can follow similar strategies if someone brings up hot-button topics that trigger your own negativity: Ask curious questions to explore the story behind their perspectives, or deflect the subject by asking a different type of question.

9. *Be appreciative.* Try not to evaluate your conversations with strangers in terms of a specific objective, such as talking for a set length of time, getting answers to a particular question, or inviting them to visit your church. Instead, think of your conversation like an expedition: You are hunting for a treasure; you just don't know what it is yet. Everyone is an expert on their own lives, with a unique perspective from their experiences. Every conversation thus offers something uniquely interesting, surprising, enriching. Look for these nuggets as your reward.

It may bring joy to express your appreciation at the end of a conversation—"Thanks for telling me about your travel in Peru. That was an amazing story." Or "I appreciate your sharing with me about what it's like to be a single parent." Or "I'm glad I learned some good gardening tips from you today!"

Journalist Celeste Headlee sums up a posture of appreciative expectation: "I keep my mouth shut as often as I possibly can, I keep my mind open, I'm always prepared to be amazed—and I am never disappointed."[5]

10. *Follow through.* Now that you've had a conversation with someone who is no longer a stranger, what comes next? If you say goodbye and never see this person again, this interaction still has value, because you got to know one of God's unique creations better.

But if your connection struck a positive chord, you can take another step toward building a relationship. Be invitational but not pushy. One option is to invite this person to a next step for connection—whether chatting over coffee (at a coffee shop or over Zoom), doing an activity together you've discovered you both enjoy, or (if you enjoy offering hospitality) inviting them to your home for a meal. Another option is to invite this person to a service or small group at your church, especially if you discover they don't have a church home. Some people have name cards printed with contact information that they can feel comfortable sharing with others, designed to be given out to invite follow-up connections.

When Things Go Wrong

Real conversations are seldom smooth sailing. Inevitably something will come out of your mouth that you wish you could take back—or the other person may say something that leaves you feeling hurt or shocked. Keep the focus on strengthening your connection.

If you offend the other person… As soon as you realize that your words have been hurtful, apologize as quickly as possible. Five hallmarks of an authentic apology: take responsibility (focus on your part of the mess); validate how they feel (focus on empathy); be genuine (speak from the heart); share how you've learned from your mistake; and affirm your desire to make things right and maintain the relationship.[6]

Avoid telling the person how you didn't intend to hurt their feelings, or what you really meant to say, or how badly you feel, or why the other person shouldn't have been offended. In Matthew 5:23-24, Jesus instructs, "If you remember that your brother or sister has something against you," then your priority is to "go, first be reconciled" to them. The other person's feelings, not your intention, are what matters to the relationship in this context.

For example, imagine you ask a woman you've just met when her baby is due—and she icily replies that she is not pregnant. While your reflex might be to seek a hasty exit from the conversation, a connection-oriented response might be, "Wow, that was rude of me! Please forgive me. I'm working on thinking more before I speak. I hope I get another chance to get to ask you a better question next time."

If you're not sure what went wrong... You have been trying to connect, but the other person doesn't respond the way you hoped. They give you a disapproving look, or ignore the compliment you just gave them, or suddenly end the conversation and walk off. How do you handle it?

First, don't assume it's about you. Maybe they had a lot on their mind. Maybe an innocent comment triggered an upsetting memory. Maybe they aren't feeling well. Or maybe the person is an introvert who just needs some alone time. Try not to take it personally.

Next, get more information. The only way to really know what is going on with the other person is to ask. Something like: "It looks to me like there might be something upsetting you. Is there anything that you'd like to share with me?" (The answer may be no.) Or, "I'm the kind of person who is thankful to be told if I say anything hurtful without meaning to."

If you believe the person may no longer want to engage, offer a graceful exit: "Thanks for talking with me, but I have to get going now. I'd enjoy visiting again sometime."

Not everyone will be receptive to forming or deepening a connection. That's OK. Show kindness anyway. "Spiritual kindness is, at its core, offering people acceptance, as well as a little of our time and attention when they are with us, no matter what their response to us may be."[7] Ask God to lead you to another opportunity for relationship.

What if you are offended? Consider your options to balance your needs and your goals for the relationship.[8] Can you let this person's comments

---

Stranger Safety

As children we learned about "stranger danger." This may be one of the deep-seated reasons we avoid talking to strangers. And sadly, there are good reasons for this caution.

In learning to talk with strangers, also promote good judgment. Expect the best from people—but be alert for red flags and stay prepared to protect yourself and others, just in case. Avoid unnecessary risks. For example, don't meet with a stranger alone in a home or other private space. For more safety guidelines, see Appendix 1.

go, without festering resentment? What could be gained by getting curious about their perspective? How might it impact your relationship to be candid about your feelings (with awareness that this makes you more vulnerable)? What do you want from this person to make things right? Remember, you can always choose to pray for this person (Matthew 5:44).

But I'm an Introvert!

A cartoon depicts a person with the label "extrovert." With a sad expression, this person is thinking, "I'm staying in tonight." The next panel shows a person labeled "introvert," grinning ear to ear and thinking, "I'm staying in tonight!"

Is talking to strangers the sole domain of extroverts, who get energized by social interaction and naturally thrive on stepping out to meet new people? We maintain that introverts, who prefer being alone or in the company of a few close friends, still have an important role in relational ministry. Introverts may find it draining to make new friends, but they bring exceptional gifts to this challenge.

Depth. "In general, introverts like people as much as extroverts do. But they enjoy them best a few at a time."[9] Once an introvert can narrow down their focus to one person, they are more likely than an extrovert to stay attentive to that person. Introverts generally prefer meaningful dialogue over small talk and are comfortable with a slower pace of engagement, which can lead to a deeper relationship.

Openness. Introverts often have a rich inner life that offers a reflective perspective. They may project a more self-aware, non-judgmental presence, which encourages others to feel free to open up. Introverts may create a more welcoming space for other introverts, who may be more guarded around an energetic extrovert.

Listening. Introverts are internal processors—they tend to think things through before they talk. Thus they tend to give others room to express themselves. "My listening abilities as an introvert are probably the greatest gift that I have to offer people," says Adam McHugh, author of *Introverts in the Church*. "In our culture people so rarely have the experience of being truly listened to—having their words, feelings, and experiences taken seriously."[10]

Friendship. Introverts take relationships seriously and tend to be more choosy about who they call a friend. Introverts express friendship with sincerity and keep friendships with loyalty. Thus, when they do form a bond of friendship with someone new, it is highly valued.

So, introverts—you are not off the hook for talking with strangers. In fact, you are needed more than ever. Overcoming social isolation in our communities will require people like you who appreciate the significance of being with others and can offer safe space for a real connection as it slowly unfurls.

The Fruit of Talking with Strangers

I (Heidi) met my best friend in college at a welcoming party for new students, when I said hello and remarked that I liked her cat earrings. Of course, not all encounters lead to a second conversation, let alone a lifelong friendship. But there is value in making the effort. You may never know how God has been at work in your conversation.

Our work of getting to know people, and laying the foundation for new friendships, is modeled after Jesus, and so we can trust it will be fruitful: "I have called you friends, because I have made known to you everything that I have heard from my Father. You did not choose me but I chose you. And I appointed you to go and bear fruit, fruit that will last" (John 15:15-16).

Notes

1. While the focus of this chapter is not conversations specifically for the sake of evangelism, see resources such as D. Scott Hildreth and Steven McKinion, *Sharing Jesus Without Freaking Out: Evangelism the Way You Were Born to Do It* (Nashville: B&H Academic, 2020); David Geisler and Norman Geisler, *Conversational Evangelism: Connecting with People to Share Jesus* (Eugene, OR: Harvest House, 2009).

2. A great resource on moving beyond small talk is Scott Doust and Abigail Doust, *Authentic Conversations: Unlocking Your Ability to Connect with Others* (McKinney, TX: McKinney Publishing, 2020).

3. Stephen Covey, *The 7 Habits of Highly Effective People: Powerful Lessons in Personal Change* (New York: Simon & Schuster; 1989), 251.

4. David Brooks, "Nine Nonobvious Ways to Have Deeper Conversations," *The New York Times* (November 19, 2020).

5. Celeste Headlee, "Ten Ways to Have a Better Conversation," TEDxCreativeCoast (May 2015).

6. See Anna Goldfarb, "What to Do When You've Said the Wrong Thing," *The New York Times* (August 18, 2019).

7. Robert J. Wicks, *Everyday Simplicity: A Practical Guide to Spiritual Growth* (Notre Dame, IN: Sorin Books, 2000), 144.

8. See Mark Merrill, "Ten Ways to Respond When You've Been Offended," Mark Merrill blog (2020), www.markmerrill.com/10-ways-to-respond-when-youve-been-offended.

9. Amy Simpson, "Confessions of a Ministry Introvert," Amy Simpson blog (September 24, 2018), https://amysimpson.com/2018/09/confessions-of-a-ministry-introvert-part-1/.

10. Adam McHugh, "Introvert? No Apology Required" (interview), Christianity.com (July 13, 2012). See also his book *Introverts in the Church: Finding Our Place in an Extroverted Culture* (Downers Grove, IL: InterVarsity Press, 2017).

4

Everyone Should Have a Friend at Church

Strengthen Authentic Connections within the Congregation

Being Friendly Is Good, but Not Enough

Years ago, I (Heidi) shared in our church's prayer time that one of our kids faced a serious challenge. Right away, one of the members took out a sheet of paper, made a chart, and quietly passed it around the congregation. Soon I was handed a list of time slots with names beside each one, so we could know that someone from the church would be praying for our kid every hour. I felt so cared for.

Church friendships are immensely rewarding. Church friends greet one another warmly each week, chat over coffee and doughnuts, share condolences and congratulations, and go out of their way to provide care in a crisis, as Heidi's church friends did. These congregational bonds enrich our spiritual, physical, mental, and emotional health.

Yet, most of us would likely acknowledge a desire for deeper relationships in our congregations. In a LifeWay survey taken August 2020, one in four pastors identified relational needs as the top challenge faced by their congregation. Over half said their church was rethinking the way members connect with one another. Even in churches not experiencing flat-out conflict, real connections may be limited in a number of ways.

Except for Sunday mornings and mid-week church activities, *church friends may not be involved in one another's lives.* We see only what is presented at church, not necessarily what families are going through day to day.

Conversations at church can be fairly shallow. We might not know one another's life stories, big questions, and dreams. We might avoid topics that are likely divisive or uncomfortable.

Members may mistake familiarity for connectedness. They may greet people in passing, or even sit beside them at Bible study every week, without ever really getting to know them. People may be friendly without making real friends.

The social circles at church may be closed to newcomers and people who don't seem to "fit in." Some people might come and go week after week without anyone interacting with them.

I (Heidi) did a project on single-parent-family ministry, and what stood out to me was how many of these parents hungered for adult connection yet felt alienated from church life. One single mother said something in a focus group that I will never forget: "I have never felt more alone in my life than sitting alone in church."

Our churches can be places where no one has to feel alone. In this chapter we share a variety of strategies for strengthening the breadth and depth of connections in the congregation. It is our dream that everyone can have real friends—and make new friends—at church.

Invite Newcomers into Connection

Creating opportunity for connections can start the moment people visit your church for the first time. Your church can consider these questions:

• How can we make people feel welcome and personally valued every time we come together?

• Who is looking out for people who don't have anyone to sit with or talk to at church?

• What structures or traditions help newer people meet and get to know others in the congregation?

• How do we learn about the hopes and preferences for connection with new people?

• What barriers to connection might be invisible to "regulars"?

There are many resources available to help churches welcome new people and plug them into church activities.[1] Here we want to focus on how new folks can be included in relationships at church. Church members can contribute to being a relationally inclusive congregation in many different ways.

Break out of your group and talk to new people. It's only human to make a beeline for the people you know when in a large group setting. But try to discipline yourself to also notice people standing alone or people you don't recognize and make an effort to engage with them.

New Connections Ministry

Designated church members can volunteer to serve as agents of connection, providing a relational bridge between newcomers and established attenders. This position is ideal for individuals gifted to be outgoing, observant, and empathetic. The role of members in this ministry:

• Notice new people or anyone sitting alone and not interacting with others.

• Introduce themselves and offer to sit nearby during the service (with awareness that some people prefer sitting alone).

• Talk with newcomers, learn a little about their story, and answer their questions.

• In future weeks, watch for these folks and greet them by name if they return.

• As newcomers get to know people, offer to introduce them to other church attenders who might be a natural connection—a family with kids the same age, someone who works in a similar job or lives in the same neighborhood, someone who shares the same hobby.

A goal for this ministry might be that after attending for several weeks, every new person would know at least three church members by name and would have at least one invitation from a church member to a meal or other social activity.

Break bread together (see Acts 2:46). If you can, gather regularly with others from church for lunch or Sunday dinner, and make it a goal to invite a guest.

Think "plus one." If you are planning a social event with another church member, also invite someone who is newer or less connected. Kids can be encouraged to do this as well.

Be a matchmaker. As you get to know people, think about what groups or networks in the church might be a good fit for them and help them make the connection.

Encouraging the congregation to be more intentional about connecting with newcomers may have the added benefit of inspiring established members to be more intentional about strengthening connections with one another as well.

Create Groups with a Relational Purpose

One of the most impactful things your church can do to encourage meaningful connections in the congregation is develop small groups. It's ideal to have some stable groups that allow people to influence one another's lives deeply over time, and some new groups that are constantly being formed or reshuffled. That's a practical way of getting new people connected while enabling different combinations of people to get to know each other.

Connection groups (also called life groups, affinity groups, or micro-communities) bring a small number of individuals or families together on a regular basis for the purpose of building "friendships that will spur them towards Christ."[2] Often meeting in homes, gatherings typically include food, sharing time, and prayer for one another, keeping up with one another's goals, joys, and struggles. The group may have an emphasis on helping one another live out their faith in their daily lives.

Connection groups can be organized as affinity groups that bring people together around what they have in common. These groups are great for welcoming new people into a circle of relationships, because it creates an instant connection.

Examples of Affinity Groups

Life experience groups are for those with similar circumstances (veterans, living with a disability) or life stage (new parents, retirement).

Vocation groups help people in the same field explore the connection between their faith and their work (social workers, entrepreneurs).

Place-based groups bring together people in the same neighborhood or apartment building, or at a college.

Activity groups build connection around doing something people enjoy (cooking, hiking).

Issue groups bring people together to learn about a complex social issue (immigration, environmental concerns) and explore where they fit in.

Intentionally intergenerational or multicultural groups are another option,[3] bringing diverse people together to build relationships. These kinds of groups can be places for rich conversations about personal history, values, faith journeys, and life experiences. The outcome can be friendships between people who might not have naturally gravitated toward each other at church, because many church activities are focused on age or life stage.

A number of years back, I (Joy) was in a group that included several families with little kids (like ours at the time), but also a recently widowed woman in her sixties and a man in his eighties who had fought in World War II. We had incredible conversations about how the world had changed, what dating was like back when, the challenges of parenting, and navigating aging.

While they may have other aims as well, such as Bible study or community involvement, connection groups keep personal relationships at the core of their purpose. (See chapter 10 for other group-based ministries.)

Strengthen Relational Aspects of Existing Church Groups

In addition to forming new connection groups, a second strategy is to use existing groups to strengthen connections. Any church group—choir, church council, Sunday school, Bible study, trustees, outreach committee, sewing circle—can become more intentional about helping the people who are involved to get to know one another better. Even if these groups are task-oriented, they can incorporate a focus on the people doing the work and create space for personal interaction.

The most basic step, which we touch on throughout the book, is to build time into regular group meetings for personal sharing. This is easier to do when groups meet in person, but with a little extra planning, online meetings can be relationally oriented as well. (For more on leading this focus on relationships in church groups and activities, see chapter 11.)

Anticipate resistance from members who assume "relational" means (as some put it) getting "touchy-feely." Building connections doesn't always involve deep emotional sharing, though it may lead there. In the context of committees and task groups, being relational may simply mean getting to know more about a person beyond the role that they play in the group. It means creating opportunity for people to discover what they have in common, or to get curious about their differences. This simple shift in the way you do the work of the church can open the door to all kinds of conversations and deeper connections.

See which of the ideas on p. 42 might be worth trying in your church's current groups. Different connection strategies might work best for different groups.

Other Opportunities to Build Connections

Any church gathering can provide an opportunity for personal interaction. For example, you could start annual congregational meetings by supplying a conversation starter and asking people to pair off to share their responses. Or take a break at some point in the meeting for a mixer exercise—provide getting-to-know-you questions, and invite members to get up and find someone they don't know well, and get to know them.

Another strategy is to set up short-term service projects that involve small teams of people working closely together. This is especially helpful if you have a lot of do-ers (people who are action-oriented) in your church. Examples might include putting together and delivering care packages, creating craft items to donate, or doing outdoor projects such as landscaping or

Ideas for Adding an Interactive, Relational Focus to Meetings
For suggested questions that groups can use to encourage personal interactions, see Appendix 2.

Opening question. Start meetings or activities with a question—a fun icebreaker, or a more personal question that can be answered briefly. Set a time limit for sharing, then move on with the meeting agenda.

Sweet and sour/Roses and thorns. Everyone has the opportunity to share a high and low point of their day or week.

Three words. If the group is large or time is a factor, start by inviting each person to say just three words that reflect what is on their heart and mind as they come to the meeting.

120. Go around the table and give each person 120 seconds to share whatever they want with the group (or pass), with no commentary.

Quirky question jar. A few times during a long meeting, stop to pick someone to briefly answer a question from the jar. Get creative with questions like: *What's the weirdest thing you've ever eaten? What do you miss most about being a kid? What event in your life would make a good movie?*

Show and tell. Give each person a hunk of clay, pack of crayons, or colorful pipe cleaners at the beginning of the meeting, and invite them to create something that expresses their state of mind. At the end of the meeting people can share with the group about what they created.

Appreciations. End meetings by inviting each person to say something they appreciate about the person next to them.

Change the setting. From time to time hold your meetings at a member's home, a restaurant or coffee shop, a picnic area, or other casual location that is more conducive to informal interaction.

building a wheelchair ramp. The key is to encourage these project teams to pray and share together as they do their service work.

Consider how to encourage connections through special events for the congregation. Some types of activities are particularly fruitful for fostering relationships. There are endless ideas for one-time events designed for socializing: dominoes marathon, scrapbooking session, chili cook-off, banquet, talent show. Even church events that are not primarily about socializing (such as a congregational prayer meeting or a concert) can include opportunities for building connections. As discussed earlier, try to start with personal interactions (and as needed, introductions and an ice breaker), and find ways to work in times for conversation as part of the activity.

As you plan how to maximize opportunities for connections in your church calendar, consider activities that:

• Involve pairs or small groups of people, versus crowds where individuals can remain anonymous.

• Engage people as active participants, instead of passive spectators.

• Are designed for introverts as well as extroverts (allow individuals to take extended time for conversation with one or two others, rather than always mixing things up).

• Have intergenerational appeal.

• Include one or more of these components that naturally encourage connection: eat, play, pray, work.

Consider how the layout of your church might enhance or detract from fostering connections.[4] To the extent allowable by your facilities and resources (as well as the ability to meet safely in the building), do you have spaces that encourage relaxed, face-to-face conversation? What setting would allow parents to socialize while they supervise their kids' play?

For a change of pace, set up stations in the narthex or fellowship area with simple, fun activities (a puzzle table, a coloring table, a cookie-decorating station, a small carnival game) to encourage members to stop and spend time with one another, rather than rushing out the door.

Fostering Relationships Online

While nothing can replace in-person worship, many churches are realizing the advantages of keeping an online dimension to church life. For example, having an online presence allows members who have moved away to reconnect with the congregation. Members may get to interact with online visitors from all over the world. In addition, people whose schedules prevent them from attending on Sunday morning now have more options for experiencing the worship service.

However, merely watching services online can make people feel even more anonymous and distanced. Beyond broadcasting their activities, churches can be intentional about using online resources as a tool to invite and strengthen connections. This is especially the case for younger generations, who interact online as a matter of course. From their perspective, by doing more socializing online, the church is just catching up with them!

Our "new normal" is that church life is likely to remain a hybrid of in-person and online. Many people have discovered that they like some aspects of doing church online, while desiring physical connection in other areas. In other words, people like having options—so try to plan relational activities that work both in person and online. The key is to be intentional about building relationships in whatever medium you are using.

Ideas for Churches to Build Connections Using Online Resources

- Weekly informal Zoom times facilitated by church leaders, just for checking in, hanging out, and prayer
- Online social activities (e.g., yoga session, book study, watch party, "meet my pet")
- Virtual game nights, with gaming tournaments or apps that involve interactive free play
- Round robin sharing in a small group via texts, email, or videos
- Private Facebook group pages for members to post updates, pictures, needs, prayer requests
- "Share my skill" classes online, where church or community folks can teach something they are good at doing (e.g., how to prepare a special dish, complete a craft, or learn Tae Kwon Do moves)

Encouraging Deeper Connections

We church people are generally nice, friendly people who have life mostly together. At least, that's the image we prefer to project.

To be fair, this is not unique to church members. Most of us go through life with a well-landscaped exterior that keeps others at arm's distance from the mess within.[5] But there is something about church that presents a challenge to getting past surface-level niceness, to authentically sharing life together. In the metaphor introduced in the first chapter, many church folks enjoy the coffee house stage of connection, may need a nudge to move toward living room connections, and prefer to stay out of the laundry room. It takes special effort to "get real" with others in the congregation—to move from being comfortably familiar and friendly, to a deeper friendship.

Being laundry room friends means making time for one another, showing up when they need you, and asking for help when you need them. A real church friend is someone you trust with all your questions and doubts as your faith meets the messiness of the real world.

Churches have options to encourage deeper, more impactful connections. Just bear in mind that not everyone wants—or is ready for— vulnerable, transparent relationships, and they can't be forced.

Strategies to encourage deeper relationships include:

Retreats. Getting away from daily routines, preferably someplace with a beautiful natural setting, encourages openness. Retreats create space for casual acquaintances to bloom into friendships. People may spend more time interacting in one weekend retreat than they would in several years of Sunday mornings.

Storytelling project. Ask life story questions and discover something new about a church member you may have known for years. Perhaps focus on exploring the stories of one particular group of people in the church. At one church, for example, youth interviewed their elders, then presented their life stories to the rest of the church. (See life story questions in Appendix 2.)

Care buddies: Two to four members commit to checking in with one another regularly, perhaps meeting for coffee or a meal, or connecting online. Care buddies pray for one another, share biblical encouragement, do small acts of kindness for one another.

Mentoring friendship. Seek out someone who has had a similar life experience (such as following the same career path, or also raising a child with autism), or build an intergenerational connection.[6]

Circle of five. Select five people you trust and invite them to be part of your support circle. This means they give you permission to contact them if a crisis arises, when you are feeling lonely or blue, or when you need prayer or advice. It also means you are willing to do the same for each of them. This can be especially helpful for people who don't have close family in the area.

Connecting with Isolated or Disengaged Church Attenders

Most congregations have people who attend services irregularly and rarely take part in church programs. Some don't participate because they prefer not to, for various reasons; others would like to be more connected with the congregation but can't because of health, disability, work schedule, family stress, or other barriers.

A group needing special attention is young adults, who are the demographic most likely to disappear from church life. One study found that about 20 percent of those who stop attending say it is because they did not feel connected to others in the congregation.[7]

Much of church life is naturally designed around the needs and gifts of active regular attenders. Yet folks on the margins are equally important. Congregational "insiders" can reach out in simple but powerful ways to make this connection.

Pay attention. A starting point in relating with people on the margins of church life is to take notice of them. When they are present, make an effort to learn their names and have a conversation. Show appreciation for something that makes them special.

Go to them. Why not get in touch with someone who rarely comes to church activities, and ask if you can meet them in a video chat or in person, at their home or wherever they prefer? Have a conversation that focuses on the person, not their church involvement.

Address obstacles to connection. Sometimes there are practical reasons limiting in-person participation, like needing transportation or childcare, that can be resolved with a little help.

Send a note. "We were just thinking of you today. How are you doing? If you'd like a call or a visit, or if you'd like to share a prayer request, let us know."

Reach out virtually. Some people find it easier or preferable to participate in church life virtually (e.g., those with small children, a long commute, or social anxiety). Be intentional about interacting with people who connect with the congregation only online.

Check on their well-being. Sometimes people miss out on church because they are facing a crisis situation. Make it simple for people to share their struggles, with a confidential online link and number to call or text. Specifically invite people to share mental health concerns.

Explore their strengths and interests. Ask questions to learn about what interests them, what skills they have, how they would want to contribute and be involved.

Include people in opportunities to bless others. For example, invite those who are homebound to write Facebook birthday messages to parishioners on behalf of the church; or write notes of appreciation to those who serve the community (teachers, health care providers, fire fighters), which the church could mail.

A Relationship-Centered View of Church Life

Many see church as the place where they get together with their friends. Sometimes this leads to the critique of church as being a social club. But if God created us to be wired for connection, what's wrong with being a social club—at least as part of what church is about? God's purpose for the church includes building and enjoying relationships. Our churches should be the most hospitable, joyful, challenging, outgoing, and deeply engaging social clubs anyone could hope for.

The problem comes when this club is exclusive and values connections with some more than others. Perhaps only those like "us" are welcome into the club. Perhaps people keep relationships at surface level because if they are their authentic selves, they fear they might be shown the door. James 2:1-9 warns against all kinds of favoritism.[8] This means *everyone* in the congregation belongs to the "in" group, and all gifts are recognized and valued.

We encourage a vision of the church as an ever-widening community of believers, growing in our relationship with Christ and friendships with one another, and always seeking ways to invite new people to connect.

Notes

1. See online resource guide for selected references.

2. Todd Engstrom, "What Makes a Missional Community Different?" The Gospel Coalition (June 5, 2013), http://toddengstrom.com/2013/06/08/what-makes-a-missional-community-different-the-gospel-coalition/.

3. See Douglas Avilesbernal, *Welcoming Community: Diversity That Works* (Valley Forge, PA: Judson Press, 2016) for guidance on strengthening connections among diverse groups in the congregation.

4. See Joseph R. Myers, *Organic Community: Creating a Place Where People Naturally Connect* (Grand Rapids, MI: Baker Books, 2007).

5. See Bill Thrall, Bruce McNicol, and John Lynch, *TrueFaced: Trust God and Others with Who You Really Are* (Colorado Springs, CO: NavPress, 2004).

6. See Karen Foster, *Lunch with Loretta* (Wheaton, IL: Crossway, 2020) for a story of life-changing conversations with a respected spiritual mentor.

7. Griffin Paul Jackson, "The Top Reasons Young People Drop Out of Church," *Christianity Today* (January 15, 2019).

8. See Jini Kilgore Cockroft, *From Classism to Community: A Challenge for the Church* (Valley Forge, PA: Judson Press, 2016).

5
Church Partnerships
Create Opportunities for Relationships in the
Broader Body of Christ

Annette handles the requests for emergency assistance at Emanuel Lutheran Church in Hutchinson, Kansas. After offering people what aid her church could provide, she would refer them to other churches and agencies that might also be able to help. Then Annette attended a community event where she got to know individuals from other churches and agencies who, like her, handled relief assistance. Before, these people had been names and phone numbers on a list; now, they began developing personal connections, which led to more collaborations.

To support one woman with complex needs, Annette helped organize a care team made up of colleagues from several churches. They worked together for months to help her with her goals for a better life. One day, several team members met with the woman at her home for a deep discussion. This led her to make an important critical personal breakthrough. It was a joyful moment. Marietta, a Mennonite, responded to this turning point by raising her hands and enthusiastically praising the Lord.

Carolyn, who is Catholic, shared an observation: "We Catholics don't usually raise our hands like that!" Marietta answered with a smile, "Most Mennonites don't either!"

Carolyn reflects on her experience with this multi-church team: "The work was extremely challenging at times, but in the midst of it, we had fun getting to know one another. We learned so much, and our friendships grew so strong. If I ever need anything, I know I could count on every one of them."

Making Connections in the Body of Christ

Partnering with other congregations in your community is a way to build bridges and expand your church's circle of connections.

As churches come together for work or worship and get to know one another in the process, they can replace suspicion and competition with bonds of unity among God's people. Partnerships provide a public witness to the broader community that people of faith are willing to set aside their differences and come together for a greater purpose. Church partnerships can also address critical community issues, pooling resources and people for greater impact.

Another benefit: connecting with Christians from other traditions and cultures can provide your church with a more full and rich experience of the body of Christ. You may expand your perspective on worship and learn about beautiful cultural traditions from all around the world. You might experience new music, new forms of community outreach, new ways of ministering to children.

I (Joy) have found that having a broader view of the whole Christian community makes me more faithful and committed to my small part of it. If I can see more of the whole thing, I am inspired by the difference that each church makes as we follow Christ in our daily lives.

Church partnerships are most beneficial when they are first and foremost about relationships. Everything you do should include an opportunity for members of different churches to meet, get to know each other better, and then build on that so that friendships can develop.

Time for meaningful interaction is valuable and won't necessarily just happen—you need to be intentional about creating it. For example, if you are doing service projects together, add in a debriefing time at the end when the group can reflect on their experience. Or if your churches are co-sponsoring an event or program (like a concert or Vacation Bible School), make sure your joint planning sessions have plenty of icebreaker exercises and opportunities to talk one on one.

As emphasized in earlier chapters, a vital step in developing relationships across congregations is to ask questions and listen to each other. When members from different churches come together, devote time for people to talk about themselves, their congregations, and what they value. Conversation starters like these could create lively discussion and help people get to know each other:

- Which ministries at your church are you involved in and why?
- What's the most exciting thing that's happened at your church in the last year?
- What are your dreams for your church in the next five years—what do you hope for?
- What's a passage of Scripture or a song from church that is important to you?

Whenever churches get together, find ways to mix up the groups so that everyone has the chance to interact with people from the other congregation. Otherwise, people from the same church sit together. (If people in your church tend to be shy, use chapter 3 in this book to build confidence in talking with strangers.)

One idea for keeping the relational focus is to form a team that includes people from both churches who meet regularly to build relationships. This mixed team can be out front together at activities sponsored by the churches. This will model to church members the possibility of building relationships and may inspire more members to get involved in the partnership.

Being in a church partnership means to bear one another's burdens (Galatians 6:2)—to care about the things that affect your partner most deeply. If your partner church is dealing with significant challenges, either within the congregation or in their community, be sensitive to their concerns. Some examples:

- The graduation rate at the local high school has been dropping
- Members of the congregation have been deported.
- The aging congregation has difficulty affording and using technology.
- The church building has a leaky roof and other costly problems.

Your church shouldn't feel it needs to step in and resolve all your partner's issues. But we think you should at least express your support and offer to be part of the conversation in figuring out what to do. You can also do the work within your congregation of raising your awareness and understanding of the issues causing your friends at your partner church to struggle. Also seek to learn about their strengths, gifts, and resources. Aim for a partnership that is asset-based and reciprocal, in which both churches give to and receive from the partnership.[1]

What Could a Relationship with Another Church Look Like?

Sometimes churches come together for an event or a cause and then make the intentional decision to build a relationship. Other times the desire for relationship comes first. Once you have reached out to make a connection, where do you take the partnership? There are countless options. First spend time together and listen to each other, so you can understand each other's values, strengths, and interests. Then be creative. Your first joint ventures don't have to be about changing the world. Find something to start with that generates enthusiasm and brings the fun! Then build on that as you move forward.

If you are planning to work together to address a concern in the community, we recommend starting by conducting a joint community listening process to learn more about needs, issues, and assets in the area (see the online resource guide for more information on how to do this).

Below are some ideas for activities you could do together.

Deepen the Connection

• Clergy and staff from partner churches can meet regularly for resource sharing, prayer, and support.

• Have a pot luck meal; everyone can bring a favorite dish from their childhood and talk about it.

• Form crafting circles (knitting, woodworking) open to anyone in the churches or in the community.

Share Church Experiences

• Send groups to visit one another's worship services or hold a joint worship service with a social time afterwards.

• Send volunteers from one church to another to help with special events or ministry programs.

• Invite the other congregation to church events such as performances of sacred music, youth group activities, or prayer meetings.

Co-sponsor Events

• Run a family camp together—a great opportunity for families in the two churches to get to know each other.

• Work together on a community event, such as a park clean-up day or community festival.

• Collaborate on a supply drive for a local school or organization.

Jointly Lead Programs

• Do a joint summer Vacation Bible School—draw a larger group of kids to the program and reduce expenses by collaborating.

• Sponsor a refugee family together, helping them get the resources and support needed to transition to life in the United States.

• Co-host a resource for people struggling with addiction, such as Celebrate Recovery or AA.

This is far from an exhaustive list. What is important is that you and your church partner discover together how you want to build on your connection.

Bringing Multiple Churches Together

Partnership can be extended across a network of churches. The challenges of coordinating activities and building real connections (not just doing tasks together) are greater, but the options for partnerships are also expanded.

Connect in Groups

• A group for pastors, or for staff in parallel positions (music directors, youth ministers, etc.), meeting regularly for mutual support and ideas.

• Christian vocational groups—an association of Christians from various churches in a particular field, like health care, education, or civil service.

• Multi-church community prayer-walking teams—walking a route in pairs or small mixed groups while praying God's blessing on the neighborhood.

• Neighborhood Bible study, for Christians from various churches who live in the same area.

Connect through Events

• Co-sponsor arts programming, such as a children's theater production, concert series, dance classes, or an arts crawl (people moving from church to church to view art).

• Plan a fun social event in which members from various churches give short, lively demonstrations of a craft or skill, or tell amusing stories from their lives, accompanied by snacks.

• Take turns hosting roundtables on a theological or social question, with people from different churches seated around each table, for the purpose of listening to one another's perspectives.

Connect through Ministry

• Organize a service day once or twice a year, with combined church teams working with nonprofits and residents to do projects in the community.

• Form a dedicated cluster to take on a bigger project, like building a house or a public playground together.

• Jointly sponsor a community social worker to work with people who approach churches seeking assistance or develop a coordinated system of benevolence.

Build Networks

- Form a network of churches prepared to provide disaster relief.
- Work together on a community organizing effort to mobilize residents to address an area of need or injustice.
- Join a coalition to learn together about mental health, childcare, or other complex issue, and explore options for a multi-church (or multi-sector) collaborative project.

In Hutchinson, Kansas, a group of people from churches and agencies concerned about poverty (including Heidi's church) decided to try a relational approach. Instead of diving in with the question, "What should we do?" we started out by getting to know one another through a series of monthly conversations over lunch. Participants shared their frustrations and hopes, and listened to people describe their personal experiences with poverty.

Out of this focus on building trusting relationships, projects emerged that we never could have predicted (such as the care team described at the beginning of the chapter). For example, in 2020, nearly two dozen churches collaborated in a food drive that delivered almost four tons of food to the community food bank. Beth, the organizer, says that personally knowing people from each of the churches made it relatively easy to put the idea into action—since trust had already been built, everyone quickly got on board.

Where to Find Church Partners

Here are a few places to look for potential church partners.

Churches in your denomination. Keep your eyes and ears open at denominational gatherings for potential partners—for example, perhaps another pastor gives a presentation on mentoring, which is an interest of your church as well. If you are seeking to partner with a congregation of a different demographic or cultural makeup, finding that diversity within your own denomination may be ideal.

Churches in your immediate geographic area. We think there is a powerful witness when churches in the same area come together to address issues, respond to crises, share in prayer and worship, and create opportunities for the community to gather.

Networks of churches. Your community may have a council of churches or ministerial alliance. Often these groups organize service opportunities, such as a community paint-a-thon, that may give your church members the chance to meet volunteers from other churches. Ministerial alliances bring clergy together to pray and discuss ministry challenges, so they offer rich potential for your pastor to find another pastor also interested in a connection.

Similar ministry. Find out which churches support the same type of ministry. For example, if your church provides meals for a homeless shelter, look to see which other churches send volunteers there. If your congregation has many families involved in foster care or adoption, ask social workers to point you to another church that also cares for kids in this way.[2]

Issue-based. Track issues in the community you care about, and notice which churches are consistently involved. For example, if you are part of a community group working on health care, note which other churches are represented. If no one has organized around an issue yet, start a network and invite other churches to the table. We have seen the impact of gathering churches together to pray and talk about a shared concern—a spike in gun violence, for example, or the need for teen programs.

Members' personal networks. Individuals in your congregation may have links with other churches through a relative, coworker, or community involvement. This contact could be a bridge to a church partnership. For example, Heidi's friend was chatting with her neighbor as they were both out watering their lawns, and she mentioned that her church (Presbyterian) was starting a study to learn more about poverty. The neighbor, who happened to be a United Methodist pastor, got excited because he too had been looking for a way to get his church more involved in poverty issues. That conversation led to a multi-church poverty simulation and follow-up initiatives.

Cross-Cultural Church Partnerships

Cross-cultural church relationships anticipate the heavenly vision of worshipers gathered "from every nation, from all tribes and peoples and languages" (Revelation 7:9). Cross-cultural partnerships have the potential to bear great fruit—releasing the joy and beauty of Christians uniting together across all kinds of boundaries. They also have the potential to fail due to misunderstanding, tension between cultures, and an unwillingness to accept different ways of doing things.

For churches serious about cross-cultural partnerships, we recommend leaning on expert resources (see the resource list online). Here we offer a few thoughts on building relationships in a cross-cultural context.

As with all partnerships, the goal is for both congregations to practice mutual respect, with each partner learning from the other and valuing what the other brings to kingdom work. You may need to do some research to discover what "respect" looks like in the other culture. In some cultures, asking personal questions shows your interest in the other person; in other cultures, it is considered a disrespectful intrusion. In some cultures calling the pastor by their first name is an indication of friendship; in other cultures, even close friends show respect by using the pastor's full title in public.

You'll also need to investigate cultural norms for interactions involving differences in gender, age, and status. Can married people and singles be put together in a small group? What are expectations for connections involving people of different generations or different genders? Is it OK to discipline another family's child? It's great if you can connect with a "cultural informant," someone from that culture who can be your guide and answer questions as they arise.

Expect to mess up somewhere along the way. A real connection doesn't mean being perfect, but being willing to learn and do better. Be patient and show lots of grace.

Where there are strong cultural differences, it's important to highlight your shared faith and discover what else you have in common. For example, Trinity Church in Indianapolis sought to connect with a church founded by Congolese refugees. Despite many differences, there were two things both congregations loved: food and music! The partnership began with church leaders and their families talking over dinner. Then about a dozen members from each congregation met for a potluck lunch. They also enjoyed an evening of worship music, with performers from both churches showcasing their different styles.[3]

Relational ministry demands a level of flexibility and tolerance for the messiness of life, even more so when cultural differences are involved. We advise against starting out with activities that require careful planning, or a rigid structure, or where there is pressure to make the event a success. Keep things simple and focused on the people, not the program. Celebrations of cultural traditions or holidays are popular, as are simple, kid-friendly community service experiences.

As a final note, consider kids in the church to be one of your greatest assets for cross-cultural connections. Kids provide a natural bridge across many types of boundaries. Plus they make stuff fun.

Church Partnerships Across Race

Pursuing partnerships between predominantly white churches and churches of color has become more common in recent years as a way for Christians to take steps toward racial reconciliation and the shared work of seeking racial justice. Here, we speak to white churches with several important don'ts and dos:

• Don't assume friendliness can replace the need to deal with issues of justice.

• Don't ignore issues of race in the partnership. The elephant is not leaving the room.

• Do ask questions about racial issues, but take responsibility for your own education. Don't expect your church partner to tutor you.

• Do encourage your members who are open to addressing racial issues to be the ones building the connection.

• Don't lean on your church partner to make your ministry diverse. Build relationships, not representation.

• Don't offer to pay for everything.

• Do consider planning a conversation about race, with your partner in the driver's seat.

• Don't think you can build a real connection without ever offending your partner, or being offended.

• Do celebrate that unity in Christ brings joy that is worth the challenges.

See chapter 9 for more on conversations about race and other tough issues that can arise with church partners.

Leading Partnerships

As congregations build a partnership, it's ideal if the leaders of the churches are themselves building a personal relationship. However, we recognize this is not always possible. The focus of relational interaction may be with the lay leaders or members. Regardless, it's vital that leadership of the partnership be shared equitably. Too often, the church with the most members, financial resources, or social status steers the decisions, expecting the other church to go along.

In leading church partnerships, seemingly minor issues can become aggravating: things like not sticking to a schedule, or people not responding to messages. Our experience is that it's often the small stuff that derails partnerships. Stay determined to show grace, remain positive, and assume the best about each other.

Even churches that belong to the same ethnic culture and denomination can have different ways of doing things, and this can strain a partnership as well. A church with a decentralized, simple congregational structure may not enjoy working with a partner that has committees, boards, and even denominational staff involved in making decisions. Or one church may be very structured, wanting to plan events six months out, and be driven crazy by a partner church that is more spur-of-the-moment and often makes last-minute changes.

Deal with differences by getting curious and then listening and communicating well (see chapter 9). Make note of the things that bother or befuddle you, then turn them into questions you can ask in a non-judgmental way. You might ask, "Your church services are so much shorter (or longer) than ours. How did that tradition develop?" Or "Some of your leaders have ministry titles I haven't seen before (Prophet, First Lady, Director of Assimilation). What is the significance of those titles? What is that person's role in your church?" After listening and learning, you are better able to discuss challenges without being critical.

Good communication and coordinated decision making are also essential to leading church partnerships. Take note of the other leader's preferences, and be aware of your own. Does one leader have an authoritative style, while the other seeks consensus? Talk together about how you will make the planning process work for both parties. Work to keep your communication positive and honest. Don't let resentments fester that can undermine your relationship.

"That They May All Be One"

I (Joy) once had a speaking engagement in a town where everyone referred to "the bridge"—a physical structure that divided the town geographically but also socioeconomically and culturally. It became clear that people on one side of the bridge weren't supposed to cross over to the other side. The churches in the room were pushing back against partnering with churches on the other side of the bridge. But I encouraged them that as followers of Jesus, we need to be all about crossing those bridges.

Bridge-crossing church coalitions have emerged in many cities, such as Unite! in Atlanta. In 2003, eight churches decided to partner toward the vision of "the next generation of Atlanta reaching their God-given potential and flourishing." This has grown into a multi-cultural, multi-denominational network of more than a hundred churches, working together in local clusters toward strategic goals to impact the community.

The outward face of this network is the amazing ministry they have accomplished in their region. At the heart, it is about the relationships weaving together diverse church leaders and congregations—including a friendship between two of the founders, Chip Sweney (Perimeter Church) and Bryan White (then a pastor at Hopewell Missionary Baptist Church). Chip writes:

Common passion for the cause of community transformation was the pilot light that ignited our friendship. . . . As a black man and a white man doing ministry in the South, we easily could have missed each other. That's an embarrassing fact, since our churches are only a few miles apart. As Bryan says, "I wasn't looking for a white friend." But Jesus, who leads the way in friend making, knew we needed each other. And he knew the kingdom cause we both embrace would be richer, more meaningful, in the context of our friendship.[4]

Jesus prayed that we "may all be one" (John 17:21). May Jesus lead the way in your friend-making with other congregations, as an answer to that prayer!

Notes

1. See Ronald Sider, John Perkins, Wayne Gordon and F. Albert Tizon, *Linking Arms, Linking Lives: How Urban-Suburban Partnerships Can Transform Communities* (Grand Rapids, MI: Baker Books, 2008).

2. One resource for linking churches in a community involved in child well-being and foster care is a network called CarePortal (www.careportal.org).

3. This story, and many others throughout the book, is associated with Joy's and Heidi's work with congregations in Indiana supported by the Center for Congregations (www.centerforcongregations.org).

4. Chip Sweney with Kitti Murray, *A New Kind of Big: How Churches of Any Size Can Partner to Transform Communities* (Grand Rapids, MI: Baker Books, 2011), 67, 69; see www.uniteus.org.

6
Community Connections
Build Relationships with Groups and Residents
in the Community

Many churches engage their community through programs, projects, or partnerships. This chapter aims to help churches strengthen the quality of connections with people in the community, in three ways: first, by building relationally-grounded partnerships; second, by incorporating more opportunities for relationships into your church's current community outreach; and third, by encouraging members of the church to get to know residents in the community.

We recommend starting with community listening that explores the community's needs, assets, and goals (see listening guide online). A great community listening process doesn't just provide information about the community; it brings church volunteers face to face with people in the community. For example, your team might interview the local high school principal, meet with a group of business owners, and attend a neighborhood crime-reduction meeting. Listening gets you in touch with those who are most passionate about working for change in the neighborhood. Church members who get deep into listening, even if they live across town, may develop a strong sense of attachment: "This is *our* community!"

You may also make surprising discoveries about who is living in the community. I (Joy) once worked with a church that didn't know about all of the homebound seniors living in the neighborhood until they did some door-to-door canvassing to promote an event. They found a group of hidden people who needed support and friendship—and who had knowledge about the community and a variety of skills. Discovering what is hidden can help you partner with the community in more relevant, effective ways.

Find Community Partners Interested in a
Relational Approach to Ministry

I (Joy) often suggest that churches try this when trying to figure out who might be a good partner: "Go stand on the front steps of your church and look across the street, and then up and down the street. If you can see a school, a community center, or a health care facility, you might already have the answer to the question, 'Who can we partner with for the sake of our community?'"

Joy and Heidi have written elsewhere about how to build effective community partnerships.[1] Here we offer a few thoughts on selecting partners that will be a good fit with an effort to move relationships to the center of church life. (We are not saying that these are the only types of community partners you should work with, but having at least one relationally-oriented partner can be an advantage).

First, look for partners that are interested in a collaborative relationship, not just collaborative activities. Working together to coordinate projects does not necessarily lead to significant or lasting connections. Is there a contact person at the partner organization who is willing to put extra time into developing a relationship with the church? Are there the makings of a positive personal connection with your partner from the start?

A related point is to consider whether this partner has a rational approach to its community activities. Look for groups that will provide opportunities for church members to connect regularly with people from the community—to talk, plan, and work side by side on projects that allow relationships to develop.

Third, consider a partner that aligns with the qualities and mindsets for relationships described in chapter 2. Examples might include treating all people with respect, engaging with assets not just needs, and listening to the community before taking action. These shared values will help hold your connection together even when the partnership hits bumps in the road.

Fourth, look for groups with strong ties in the community. This may lead you to look beyond nonprofits and schools, though they can make excellent partners, to consider more informal networks and associations.

Examples might include partnering with the Chamber of Commerce to jointly sponsor a summer entrepreneurship program for youth; or connecting with a book club at the library, and offering childcare and transportation so more parents can participate.

Finally, track the connections that church members already have in the community. Ask members where they volunteer, work, or serve on boards in the community, and whether they have personal contacts within these organizations that they could introduce to church staff.

Here is an example of how following a trail of connections leads to community impact. Eastminster Presbyterian Church in Simpsonville, South Carolina, partnered with a child well-being initiative called Strong Communities:

> A retired Latino couple, one of whom was a certified lay pastor, became active in the church and opened everyone's eyes to the exploitation of immigrant communities. Working with Strong Communities, Eastminster took the lead in organizing an intergenerational Latino family camp. The church called on its partnership with the local YMCA to initiate an outreach program for Latino youth to play soccer and a wellness program for Latino parents. When a federal raid on a local poultry plant left hundreds of Latino families without income or food, the community looked to Eastminster for leadership.[2]

Partnerships like this that are built around a relationship, rather than an activity, may be more flexible and responsive to a changing context.

Benefits of Relational Community Partnerships

Community partnerships bring many benefits. They extend your church's reach and impact in the community; provide your church with new ideas, expertise, resources, and people; and bring people together who care deeply about the community. For complex community issues, like gun violence or health care, partners bring the wide range of ideas, experiences, and networks needed to make an impact.

During the pandemic, we watched churches that had already developed community partnerships do more than they ever thought possible. Since they already had trusting relationships with people in the community, it was easier to bring people from church and community together to figure out what to do and then get the work done.

For example, by investing in listening, connecting with school staff, and reaching out to parents, First Christian Church of Newburgh, Indiana, built a strong partnership with two nearby elementary schools. When the pandemic hit, First Christian quickly pivoted—they helped the schools with food distribution, checked in with students' families, and bought thermometers for teachers. Two of the church's team members were invited to serve on the school's COVID planning team.

So, keep in mind: The community relationships you develop now could prove invaluable the next time your community experiences a crisis!

In addition to helping meet practical needs, partnerships can help you build relationships with people in your community you might not otherwise have the opportunity to get to know. If your church has a heart to connect with vulnerable or difficult-to-reach groups, connecting with an organization that is already trusted and established in the community opens doors. For example, partnering with an organization that works with immigrants and refugees will help you build relationships with them and learn more about their culture, history, and current situation.

Partnerships can also educate church members about community issues in a real-world way. Working side by side with people of diverse racial, economic, religious, or cultural backgrounds associated with a partner organization makes it more likely that honest dialogue can occur and friendships can develop. It is sometimes assumed that people's minds must be changed so that they will be open to new relationships. But over and over, we have seen this working in reverse—as church members develop new relationships, this opens their minds to new perspectives as a result.

I (Joy) have worked on a number of church-school partnerships over the years. Every time I went with a group of church volunteers to visit a school to see what was possible, I could see the volunteers gaining new perspective on the daily challenges facing public school staff. Talking with staff, we learned a lot—about the diversity of the student body, the struggles of students living in poverty, and what adults from the broader community could do to help. This motivated the volunteers and helped us develop programming that was relevant to the situation.

Finally, partnering helps a church to be more effective in doing good. A church that lacks expertise in complex issues like addictions, generational poverty, or mental health could hurt those they are trying to help, unless it teams up with (and listens to) organizations that do know what they are doing.

Ways of Partnering That Strengthen Relationships

Some partnerships are built around specific goals or activities. You can cultivate lasting connections while still collaborating efficiently. As you work with a community partner to accomplish ministry goals, here are ways to focus on strengthening the relational aspects of the partnership.

Make it personal. Make an intentional effort to meet staff, volunteers, and constituents of your partner face to face and get to know them as individuals. Learn about their vision, their history with the organization, what motivates them to be part of this project. And share your own vision and story.

Do listening projects together. Doing listening activities together with a community partner is impactful, especially if you are initiating something new. For example, a church member and organizational volunteer can pair up to interview other community contacts.

Plan and brainstorm together. Getting in a room (or a Zoom room) with staff and volunteers from your partner to do planning could help everyone come up with new ideas, as well as get to know each other better. The community partner may challenge the church to see things from a different perspective. You can plan together for a joint project or get one another's input on things you are going to do separately.

Connect with people served by your partner. For example, one church's high school students decided to connect with a group home for individuals with disabilities. "On a regular basis they committed themselves to being present, befriending, and loving residents with special needs in the way of Jesus." The group home then asked the church to host A Night to Shine, a prom night experience for people with special needs.[3]

Offer support. Life can be hard for everyone, and especially if your partner is a nonprofit that deals with people's struggles day after day. Check in regularly with staff and volunteers, ask how they are doing, and listen. Offer to pray with or for people. Send a note of encouragement. Have a

Partnership Stories

Calvary Lutheran Church[4] has a kitchen and members who enjoyed cooking. What could they do in the community, they wondered? How about invite the homeless shelter down the street to bring guests over to make a meal together along with members of their church, and then sit down and eat it together? It was a hit! Pastor Daryl noted, "It's not just 'our' kitchen anymore. It can be shared space."

After a brutal winter, Bethel Community Church resolved that no one should die of exposure in their community. But what could one small church do? They focused their energy on building a network of churches willing to work together to provide overnight shelter on a rotating basis, with local agencies providing food and supportive services. They also formed a group composed of people who had been homeless and volunteers, to provide feedback on the initiative as it evolved.

St. John Lutheran did a listening project in their community, thinking it would lead to a new ministry program. Instead, they discovered a need for meeting space. The church cultivated relationships with an adoption support group, a ministry for children with autism, and an elder care agency, which now regularly use their building and interact with members of the church. St. John doesn't just provide space but genuine hospitality as well.

Noting that various groups working on substance abuse in their community were not familiar with one another, Central Christian Church Disciples of Christ organized a series of town halls on recovery. Organizational representatives come together to get to know each other's role in recovery work, develop ideas for collaboration, and build trust.

celebration of ministry at the church, and invite partner staff to come and be appreciated.

Have fun together. Gather with staff and volunteers from your partner periodically to do something fun. If you can do this while enjoying community assets, like a fabulous BBQ restaurant, bowling alley, arcade, or walking trail—so much the better!

Build Connections through Current Community Programs

What if your church is already involved in a community ministry that is largely transactional in nature—meaning the ministry provides needed goods and services to people without getting to know them or interacting with them in a meaningful way? How might you incorporate some kind of relational component into this ministry?

Below are several options a church might consider for building connections, even in a small way. (The examples below are composites inspired by real-life models.)

Have conversations. This may seem simplistic, but talk to people. See chapter 3 and the questions in Appendix 2 for ideas on how to make the most out of even a short encounter. (But be sensitive—when people are in crisis is not the time to strike up a casual conversation.) *A volunteer at a local thrift store says hello to everyone; sometimes, customers stop to chat, and every once in a while, end up talking deeply about their lives. This volunteer greets repeat customers by name and asks how their child's surgery went or whether they got the job they were applying for.*

Engage in listening projects. Every encounter with a community resident is an opportunity to learn from them. Use focus groups, interviews, and surveys to get feedback on the ministry program, as well as new ideas for bettering the community and how people would like to be involved (see the community listening guide online). *A church provides free haircuts to students at a nearby elementary school. While students and parents wait in line for their haircut, they are invited to respond to a simple three-question survey on the community.*

Invite people to contribute. Build in opportunities for reciprocity based on people's gifts and capacities. Inviting those who use a service to help with the work builds connections as well as dignity. *A meal kitchen invites guests to stay afterward to help clean up. Several people consistently stay to help; and over time they have formed bonds with one another, the meal kitchen staff, and the church volunteers who come to serve the meal.*

Incorporate time for group interaction. Chapter 4 gives numerous ideas for building relational time into the start of meetings and activities. *A housing task force includes a time on its agenda for group members to share with one another why this work is important to them. A GED class closes each week with participants offering affirmations and appreciations to one another.*

Ask about gifts, assets, and interests. On program applications, in addition to standard questions about income, household, and so on, why not ask about the participant's best qualities and greatest strengths, the skills they possess, their goals for the future? *A man who had lost his job came to a church seeking help with utility bills. The church volunteer assisting him asks, "What kind of work would you like to do?" This stops him in his tracks. He says, "No one has ever asked me that before!"*

Involve people in planning and leadership. Invite individuals served by the program to collaborate with the church's ministry team. *A program that provides school supplies recruits an advisory team of students and parents to help plan lists of supplies and coordinate delivery.*

A key principle of a relational approach is to do ministry *with* people, not *to* them. This is also framed as the motto, "Nothing about me, without me." See the online resource guide for recommended sources on how to ground charitable ministry in asset-based relationships and mutuality.

Assess the Relational Qualities of Your Church's Current Community Outreach

One of the most important ways any community ministry program can encourage connections is by treating everyone involved in the ministry with respect, kindness, and encouragement. A test of whether a ministry is oriented toward real connections is whether people know they matter.

"There were times when I had to get help and I was made to feel like I was a burden, an inconvenience. It weighs on your soul," says Heidi's friend Shawna, who has been through many struggles, and now helps others (see story on p. 91). "When someone talks to you like you are a human being, it makes you feel like you have a purpose for being on this planet."

We have both witnessed community ministries where people were treated brusquely, with condescension or even suspicion. The church was in the role of rescuer, and people from the community were viewed as being either needy or greedy. It's hard to build relationships on that foundation.

One way to assess the relational qualities of a community ministry is to ask those who participate in it for their honest feedback. Another way is to try to observe it firsthand: Make an appointment to get groceries from your church's food pantry. Shadow a youth in your after-school program. You probably won't be incognito, but you'd at least get a different perspective on the program. Then reflect on the interactions you observed. What relational skills or qualities did you see in play (good listening, curiosity, an asset mindset, mutuality, availability, openness)? What steps could you recommend to strengthen the ministry from a relational perspective?

Connection Lessons from a Church Carnival

I (Heidi) took my kids and their friends to a community carnival hosted by a church a few blocks from our own congregation. Who could pass up the offer of a hot dog, a bouncy house, and prizes? The kids had a great time, but I felt increasingly uncomfortable.

• All the volunteers were wearing matching T-shirts with a message about loving the community. That visually set the church members apart from the community that was getting "loved."

• When we arrived, we were asked to register. One of the registration questions was, "Do you have a church where you attend regularly?" I observed that the people in front of us who answered "no" got one color wrist band, but we got a different color band based on our "yes" response. Immediately I felt like a freeloader. The carnival posters said all were welcome, but clearly it was intended for the neighborhood families who might be attracted to their church.

• The church volunteers running the carnival were friendly, but mainly chatted with one another. Other than offering me a hot dog, no one talked to me directly.

• While the kids enjoyed themselves, I joined the other parents who were standing around awkwardly, not talking to one another.

I found myself wondering what the carnival experience might have been like had the church invited parents from the community to join them on the planning team . . . if parents (or even kids) were helping run the games alongside church members (and no one could tell which was which) . . . if families from the neighborhood had been encouraged to mingle with one another . . . if church members had been curious to know something about me other than whether I already had a church home. What connections might have developed?

Build Connections with the People Living Around the Church

So far, we've been focusing on programs and partnerships. We close the chapter by offering a few suggestions for reaching out informally in your church's neighborhood to build personal connections. The goal is to encourage members of your congregation to get to know people living around your church.

If your church lacks this connection with the community, church members may drive through the neighborhood to get to worship services, oblivious that thanks to a plant closing, many of these residents have just become unemployed. Or that a child was killed walking home from school. Or that a group of young entrepreneurs is starting a farmer's market. Church members won't discover these things unless they get out in the community and talk to people.

Getting to know residents is especially important when the neighborhood has undergone change, and the demographics or culture of the congregation is different from that of the surrounding area. It's possible that church members have stereotypes about the neighborhood and the people who live there (or vice versa). Or the church has been involved in activism around community issues without getting to know anyone affected by the issue on an individual level. Looking beyond stereotypes and problems to build real connections breaks down barriers and changes the conversation.

Many of the suggestions you will find in the next chapter for how people can build connections in their home neighborhood could be applied in the church's neighborhood as well. Here we share a few additional strategies for fostering trust and positive connections follow.

Find the neighborhood insiders. If you are starting from a blank slate in making connections, or if the demographic makeup of the congregation is quite different from the community, a good first step might be finding a neighborhood insider who can help connect you with others. Some refer to this as finding the "person of peace," as Jesus instructed in Luke 10:6. This is someone from the community who offers you hospitality and willingly "operates as a gatekeeper, opening relational doorways into their network of relationships."[5]

Show up. Spend time in the community, prayerfully observant and open to interactions. Sit in a coffee shop. Go prayer walking. Patronize local businesses. Participate in neighborhood associations and civic councils. Take part in community events, like concerts in the park. Everywhere you go, be curious and invite conversations. Say hello to people and see who says hello back. (See chapter 3 for tips on talking with strangers.)

Do what you enjoy. The easiest way to connect with people is through shared interests. Whatever you enjoy—sports, comic books, live music—find your way to others who enjoy it too. For example, find the local restaurant that serves up the best pie and become a regular. If you love theater, get season tickets to the local community theater group, volunteer backstage, or audition for a play. What more natural way to make a new friend?

Join a community advocacy group. Personal relationships are vital to guide and sustain the work for justice (an idea Robert Linthicum develops in his book, *Transforming Power*). Plug into grassroots advocacy efforts, where church members may connect with people from diverse backgrounds pursuing the same goal.

Create forums for connection. Working with community residents, plan activities to bring people in the community together and encourage positive interaction—a block party, game night, open mic youth coffeehouse, beautification project, salsa dancing class, track and field day with activities for all ages . . .

Discover talents. Every community is home to a rich array of talents and skills. Find out what people are good at doing, and put that knowledge to good use. Knowing who makes the best cookies can come in handy when you need snacks for a church event, for example. Or you might introduce an aspiring DJ to a family planning a quinceañera. Conversations that revolve around discovering gifts and skills generate energy for new relationships.

Broadway United Methodist Church in Indianapolis has raised asset discovery to an art form. "At the center of neighbor love is curiosity—about the world and about other people. Around the church, we call this mutual delight." The book by former Broadway pastor Michael Mather, *Having Nothing, Possessing Everything,* is a stirring resource for a movement toward relationships of abundance and joy at the center of community outreach.

> When we got out of our building and opened ourselves up to receive hospitality as well as to share it, the learning and discovery expanded. Organizations and institutions can find ways, maybe just a few times a year, to put their people in the homes of the neighbors they serve. If, in gathering together, people intend to listen and to learn from one another—not about some issue, but about each other's lives and gifts—then new doors will appear and open.[6]

Behind every door in your community is a potential new connection!

Notes

1. Joy Skjegstad, *Seven Creative Models for Community Ministry* (Valley Forge, PA: Judson Press, 2013); Ronald J. Sider, Philip N. Olson, and Heidi Unruh, *Churches That Make a Difference: Reaching Your Community with Good News and Good Works* (Grand Rapids, MI: Baker Books, 2002).

2. Jill McLeigh and David Taylor, "'Bear One Another's Burdens': A Church and a Community in Transformation," *International Journal on Child Maltreatment* (2020), 3:197–210, 202.

3. Mac McCarthy, "How to Shift Small Groups to Missional Communities," Gravity Leadership (July 24, 2017).

4. To learn more about the churches and their community partnerships, visit these websites: Calvary Lutheran Church, www.calvarylutheranangola.com; Bethel Community Church, www.tribtown.com/2017/11/23/sacred_opportunity; St. John Lutheran Church, www.stjohnindy.org; Central Christian Church, www.centralchristiandoc.org.

5. Alex Absolom, *The Viral Gospel: How Finding Your Person of Peace Accelerates Your Mission* (Carolina Beach, NC: Exponential Resources, 2014), 18.

6. Michael Mather, *Having Nothing, Possessing Everything: Finding Abundant Communities in Unexpected Places* (Grand Rapids, MI: Eerdmans, 2018), 125.

7

It's a Beautiful Day When You Know Your Neighbors

Connect with the People in Your Neighborhood

I (Heidi) was returning home from a conference, about a decade ago. It was the middle of the night, I was exhausted, and the airline had lost my checked bag. I took the shuttle to the dark, deserted parking lot, found my car—and only then realized that my car key was in my checked bag. (I never made that mistake again!) At that time we had small children and my husband couldn't leave them alone while he drove an hour each way to bring me the spare key. Anyway, he was asleep and wasn't answering the phone.

What to do? I called our neighbor, April.

She listened sympathetically to my story, then swung into action. She went to our house, banged on the door to wake up my husband, and then stayed with our kids while he came to my rescue. It's beautiful to know your neighbors.

Real Connections in the Neighborhood

The pandemic underscored the timeless lesson that we don't just go to church; we must be the church, wherever we are. The ministry of the church does not center around programs and activities. It is a seamless process that happens everywhere we are willing to interact in a Christ-like way with the people we encounter, including in our own neighborhoods.

Good neighboring is a key practice for a congregation that is moving toward a focus on real connections. The "church gathered" can be the place where members are encouraged and equipped to be the "church scattered" for relational ministry with the people who live around them. Churches can offer ideas and resources for building connections with neighbors, share inspiring stories, talk about hard questions, and provide a warm welcome for neighbors invited into the congregation.

The essence of good neighboring is applying Jesus' command to "love your neighbor as yourself" to our literal neighbors. Neighboring requires no special talent except being available, appreciative, and caring, as well as being open to the nudgings of the Holy Spirit. It may look different in various types of neighborhoods—but "no matter where you live, there's a stranger who wants to become a neighbor."[1]

Meeting Your Neighbors

The first step to being a good neighbor is to get to know your neighbors. Nearly a third of Americans don't know the names of anyone who lives by them. You may be thinking, "But I rarely even see my neighbors!" Here are several ways to generate opportunities to interact beyond a smile and wave.

Get out your door. Make a plan to spend time where people can see you—yard, front stoop, porch, hallway, lobby, or courtyard. Create an inviting space for interaction—fire pit, table with Legos or jigsaw puzzle, chalkboard, lawn game, or several chairs. Leave your door open while making dinner or baking goodies, and see who comes by to see what's cooking.

Kristin Schell tells the story in *The Turquoise Table* of putting a picnic table in the front yard and making it a gathering place for conversations over coffee, crafts, and homework with kids, and multi-family picnics. It was the spark for many new relationships.

Knock on their door. It feels unnerving, but if you really want to meet your neighbors, you may have to go out to them. If it helps not to go empty-handed, take flowers or a plate of cookies. Another catalyst for knocking on doors may be sharing timely information, like a street closing or neighborhood event, or checking on neighbors after a crisis. If you and your neighbor have kids, that may be all the excuse you need.

After initial introductions, follow up with a genuine compliment (*Your roses are amazing—what's your secret?*), a question (*Since your kids are about the same age as ours, I thought I'd ask you for suggestions of fun activities?*), or use the direct approach (*I realized that we've lived on the same block for six months and I didn't know your name, so I decided to do something about that!*) See chapter 3 for more on how to strike up a conversation with neighbors you don't know well. Then you can follow up, such as an invitation for coffee and dessert.

Offer hospitality (Romans 12:13). Create a welcoming atmosphere, offer refreshments, give people a comfy place to sit, and most importantly smile and let them know you are glad to see them. Don't worry about the quality of your home décor or your cooking—the goal of hospitality is to make the other person feel important and valued, and to anticipate their needs. On a hot day, for example, hospitality can look like popsicles at the ready for kids who pass by after school, or a basket of water bottles set out beside your door, served with a greeting that invites further conversation.[2]

Learn about the neighborhood. Find someone to give you a history of the neighborhood: "Every city block or neighborhood will have an unofficial mayor. Someone who's been there a long time, likely seen a lot of change, and constantly has eyes on the street. Get to know them."[3] Talk to neighbors about other questions you may have about the neighborhood, such as the story behind a mural, or who owns an abandoned lot.

Have a party. Any excuse to throw a party or host a dinner is an excuse to invite your neighbors—even if you haven't met them yet.

Lynda MacGibbon writes about how she met her neighbors in a Toronto high rise.

> I have lived here for 16 months. I walk down the hallway at least twice a day, often more. I hear keys turn in locks, but I rarely see people. I am fortunate to have a good friend who moved in down the hall from me. We figured that knowing each other might be a good foundation for getting to know our neighbours and so we decided to throw a party for the people who live on our floor. I

went door by door, slipping invitations up against the locks, hoping I'd made them friendly enough, normal enough that people would be enticed rather than scared off by our imposition. . . .

And something amazing happened. The people who live on my floor came. They brought food and drinks. They shared their stories. They said things that were hilariously funny and we all

Connection Style	Examples
Food	BYOM (Bring Your Own Meat) backyard BBQ Bring-a-Topping baked potato or taco bar Cookie (or holiday-specific snack) exchange
Fun activities	Movie night—streaming watch party, or outdoors using a projector Game night—online or in-person games Puzzle party—set up a card table with a big picture puzzle and snacks
For kids	Play group for young children and parents Messy outdoor craft project or water games Neighborhood scavenger hunt
For teens/youth	Organize homework help or home-based after-school homework club Start a youth-led neighborhood business (pet sitting, yard maintenance) Start or join a gaming group
Listening	Ask neighbors, *What kind of a day have you had today?*—then listen Block Bingo—engage neighbors in learning about each other in the form of a game Arrange for kids to interview elders and long-term residents in the neighborhood[5]

laughed. They ate, and drank, and stayed late into the evening. And when they stood up to leave, they all said thank you. One after another, they said, "I wanted to know my neighbours." We've already set a date for the next party.[4]

Activities to Build Connections with Neighbors

Once you've met your neighbors, it takes intentional effort to develop the connection—or as the *Art of Neighboring* puts it, moving from acquaintance to relationship. Be persistent, creative, and invitational. The chart

Connection Style	Examples
Active	Go dog walking (or just walking) together Find a partner to do morning yoga online Start a pick-up soccer or basketball game
Seasonal	Spring—deliver small flower pots and a pack of flowers Summer—ice cream float party Fall—pumpkin decorating contest Winter—hot cocoa and decorating pre-baked cookies
Small groups	Home repair exchange—share tools and help each other with projects Early morning running or gym group Start a neighborhood book club—meet to discuss a book about a particular issue, and consider taking action together
Prayer	Front door prayer (pray for all the households you can see from your door) Invite a neighbor to take a prayer walk Give neighbors a prayer card: How can we pray for you this week?

on pages 78–79 offers a range of practical suggestions, many of them suitable for doing outdoors in good weather. You may need to try lots of things before finding what works in your context. The point is not just to do the activity, but to build a sense of community with your neighbors.

The suggestions on pages 78–79 may be led by one or two families. The suggestions below call for more organized neighborhood collaboration.

Service	Organize a neighborhood drive for a nonprofit (food, toiletries, or gift card) Neighborhood clean-up/art project Coordinate neighbors to visit regularly with residents who are elderly or who need help with small jobs, lawn care, snow shoveling, etc.
Community organizing	Start a neighborhood association, to address neighborhood concerns and provide a "welcome wagon" for new people moving into the neighborhood Organize a neighborhood emergency team to develop a contact list/preparedness plan Neighborhood connectivity online—set up group page on social media
Neighborhood-wide activity	Block party (work with the fire department to have a flowing hydrant turn your street into a water park) Progressive dinner (go door to door in small groups for each dish) Plant a community vegetable garden (or herb garden for indoor growing), then prepare a community meal using the produce

The best strategy is to make yourself available, be prayerfully observant, and be willing to step out and make a connection when you see the opportunity.

Luke and his wife were foreign missionaries for years, but when the pandemic hit, they were suddenly evacuated back to the U.S. Family ties brought them to the Midwest, where they chose a lower-income neighborhood to continue to live out incarnational mission among their neighbors. This took the form of fixing bikes, playing backyard games with kids, sharing snacks, and having long talks through the screen door.

"When I would see my neighbors out in their yard or walking their dog, I went out to talk with them," Luke says. "I didn't just wave hello or wait for them to come to me. In Mark 16:15, Jesus doesn't say, 'Let the world come to you and preach the gospel to all creation.' He says, 'Go into all the world. . . . ' We need to go to where people are, even if that just means crossing the street."

Benefits of Good Neighboring Relationships

Developing connections lays the groundwork for good neighboring relationships. What does this look like?

Listen to your neighbors. Having a safe, supportive person to vent to can lessen a neighbor's burdens of stress and isolation. And having someone to celebrate with makes good news all the sweeter. "Rejoice with those who rejoice; weep with those who weep" (Romans 12:15).

Give and receive help. Being a good neighbor means being available if they need a helping hand (tool, someone to watch their pets on vacation); and it means being authentic about asking for help when you need it (say, if you get stranded at the airport in the middle of the night). Being mutually trustworthy in little things may lead toward deeper levels of relationship.

Be a safety net in times of trouble: picking up a prescription for a sick neighbor; quietly leaving groceries for a neighbor who lost their job; driving a neighbor who needs protection to the domestic violence center. If you are prayerfully observant, God will lead you to be at the right place at the right time to show compassion.

Look out for kids. Children—and parents—thrive when there are lots of helpers close by to provide snacks, wise guidance, an encouraging word and a watchful eye. Especially after traumatic experiences such as the pandemic, being a positive, caring presence for the kids in your neighborhood can help them rebuild their resiliency.

It's important to respect safety guidelines when interacting with children. For example, don't invite children into your home or take them out anywhere without their parent/guardian's permission. See other suggested guidelines in Appendix 1.

Be interested in your neighbor's story. We will always find something to be annoyed about with our neighbors, but we can make an intentional shift toward empathy.

For example, Matt complained about his neighbor's weedy lawn, unkempt house, and beat-up cars, making critical assumptions about what kind of person he must be. Then God stirred Matt to invite his neighbor over to lunch. "Four simple words changed my entire perspective about my neighbor," says Matt: *Tell me your story.* Matt learned his neighbor was an immigrant who struggled with unemployment and depression. Judgment gave way to kindness, as Matt brought his church's life group over to clean up his new friend's yard.[6]

Appreciate the diversity of your neighbors. Half of Americans say they don't trust most of their neighbors.[7] You can help break down stereotypes and suspicions by creating opportunities for your diverse neighbors to spend time with one another, expanding cultural horizons and promoting mutual respect and trust. For example, host an event that highlights cultural traditions and foods. Neighborhoods where residents have strong personal relationships are better able to draw on their differences as a strength.

Work together with your neighbors. As you get to know one another, you may discover shared goals or problems you all want to solve together like improving sidewalks or lighting. As a respected connector who listens and brings people together, you can help facilitate action.

Enjoy life with your neighbors. A connected neighborhood is a place "full of boys and girls playing in its streets" (Zechariah 8:5), a place where people can relax, socialize, and have fun together. You can organize neighborhood activities such as holiday parties or team sports, or make regular time for hanging out.

Help your neighbor connect with God. Perhaps (like the authors) you've gone into hiding when a person carrying religious tracts approaches your door. That is not the approach we recommend. Yet when we know our neighbors and genuinely care for them, then this can naturally take the form of encouraging their relationship with God—as this pastor's story illustrates:

> My new neighbor Tom and I were talking in the front yard when he mentioned that he was painting murals in his children's rooms. He told me he had some community service hours to complete, and asked if there was any work he could do for our church.
>
> Not long afterward, we would be working together designing a mural depicting children running into Jesus's open arms. While Tom painted the mural at the church, we had several candid conversations about life and faith, and I had the opportunity to share from my heart about the difference a relationship with Jesus had made in my life and the lives of those I love.[8]

What could faith sharing in the context of an authentic, caring connection look like? Offering to pray for a neighbor with health problems; including neighbors in a home-based Bible study; inviting families with kids to a backyard Easter egg hunt and Resurrection celebration; listening to a neighbor who is wrestling with spiritual questions (without necessarily having all the answers). We also point others toward the gospel by being a good neighbor who models the love of Jesus: "The Word became flesh and blood, and moved into the neighborhood" (John 1:14, The Message).[9]

Build Asset-Based Neighborhood Relationships

Each of your neighbors has gifts from God, and using them to benefit others is part of God's design (Ephesians 2:10). What skills, talents and special qualities do your neighbors have that you can affirm and graciously receive?

David Sanford's *Loving Your Neighbor* shares this example of an asset-based connection:

It was just another typical day for a mom with small children. Renée managed to put a naughty young child in a time out calmly. Then to cool off she went straight to the kitchen and slammed the sturdy wooden back door. . . . This particular door had a decades-old-window that promptly broke into pieces. After getting over her initial embarrassment, Renée immediately thought of her new neighbor friend, Karen, and her husband, Ed, who did home repairs. . . .

Ed was wary of people he didn't know. Yet, when asked, Ed was more than happy to come right over to fix the window. Once he was in our house, he relaxed, met the kids and teased them, and discovered we were a friendly family too. . . . Out of that humbling "worst day" experience came a "best neighbors" friendship.[10]

An asset-based approach to neighboring spreads the net of blessing wider by connecting neighbors with one another in mutually beneficial ways. For example, you might discover that the neighbor on your left is an auto mechanic, and the household on your right has a college student with a talent for numbers. Then you can introduce these neighbors to each other when one needs their car repaired or the other has a child wanting help with algebra. Bringing neighbors together around gifts builds a stronger, more abundant community.[11]

Developing this web of asset-based relationships also helps neighborhoods get through crises together. Neighborhoods where people know, rely on, and share with one another are more coordinated and resilient in their response to traumatic events. Disaster readiness expert Linda Loosli quips that in an emergency, "That guy down the street with a chainsaw may be your new best friend."[12]

The Challenges of Neighboring

Those who set out to build connections with neighbors will face barriers similar to any relational effort: Our schedules are too full. It's risky. It feels incredibly awkward (especially for introverts). Some challenges, however, are unique to good neighboring.

First, in some neighborhoods, seeking interactions beyond a smile and wave violates an unwritten rule. "At one time, being 'neighborly' meant reaching out to the people who lived next door. . . . Today, being 'neighborly' means leaving those around you in peace."[13] We need to respect people's desire for privacy. But for every neighbor who prefers being left alone in their fortress of solitude, there are probably several who would welcome a drawbridge out of isolation. We can trust God to guide us to those neighbors most in need of a friend.

Neighboring is about "being flexible, available and present" (*The Neighboring Church*). Frankly, this sometimes means that neighboring is unpredictable, inconvenient, and time-consuming. You may have a lonely neighbor, for example, who regularly comes over wanting to talk . . . and talk. Make decisions as a household about setting boundaries. It's OK to set time limits or to hold off on bringing people into your home, especially if you have children. (See Appendix 1 on safety and boundaries.)

You may get thrown into situations with no clear rules. How to be a good neighbor to the guy whose dog poops on your lawn every day? Is giving money to a neighbor in need helpful or enabling? When and how do you step in if you think your neighbors are to harsh with their children? These questions are uncomfortable, but they are a sign you are on the right track in building real connections. It helps when others in your church are also working on neighboring, so you can help one another process the hard questions.

Another potential challenge: Many American communities are still largely segregated by class and race.[14] If the people in your neighborhood are demographically similar to you, then focusing all your connection efforts on immediate neighbors may have the effect of reinforcing this segregation. Be aware of this dynamic so you can be intentional about crossing barriers in other types of relationships. Some may even make the choice to relocate into communities where they can become neighbors with people experiencing the pain of poverty and injustice.[15]

How Churches Support Good Neighboring

Twenty pastors sat down with the mayor of Arvada, Colorado, to ask how churches could work together to serve the city. They discussed the problems in the community, like hunger, at-risk kids, substance abuse, dilapidated housing—the list went on.

Then the mayor, Bob Frie, shared his vision of a community in which "no one falls through the cracks." Frie went on to say, "You could address a lot of these problems just by teaching the people in your churches how to be good neighbors."

This conversation sparked a movement among this group of churches to become "a community of great neighbors" who looked after one another. As described in *The Art of Neighboring*, the pastors agreed to preach and teach about loving neighbors. They encouraged church members to start by learning the names of the people who lived closest to them. Members turned acquaintances into relationships by inviting neighbors over for meals, hosting block parties, listening to people's stories, having fun together, checking in on one another, showing up to help. More and more, neighboring just became a way of life.[16]

Neighboring relationships are not a panacea for needed change in a community. But they can have a broad impact. What might happen if your church encouraged everyone to truly get to know the people in their neighborhoods?

Notes

1. Allie Utley, Neighboring Movement Blog, www.neighboringmovement.org.

2. For ideas see Leslie Verner, *Invited: The Power of Hospitality in an Age of Loneliness* (Scottdale, PA: Herald Press, 2019).

3. Suggestion from a realtor, quoted in Shauna Pilgreen, *Love Where You Live: How to Live Sent in the Place You Call Home* (Grand Rapids, MI: Revell, 2019).

4. See Lynda MacGibbon, *My Vertical Neighborhood: How Strangers Became a Community* (Downers Grove, IL: IVP, 2021). The quote is from her blog at lyndamacgibbon.com.

5. See Erin Feher, "Hey Neighbor! Ten Questions to Ask the Family Next Door" (August 5, 2018), https://redtri.com/hey-neighbor-10-questions-to-ask-the-family-next-door. Also see questions for Intergenerational Neighborhood Interviews in Appendix 2.

6. Matt Svajda, Neighborhood Initiative blog (August 3, 2019), neighborhoodinitiative.com. Mr. Rogers reportedly carried a note in his pocket with this wisdom: "You'll never meet a person you can't learn to love once you've heard their story."

7. George Gao, "Americans Divided on How Much They Trust Their Neighbors," Pew Research Center *FactTank* (April 13, 2016), https://www.pewresearch.org/fact-tank/2016/04/13/americans-divided-on-how-much-they-trust-their-neighbors/.

8. "Loving Your Neighbor through Prayer," Our Daily Bread, https://ourdailybread.org/resources/loving-your-neighbor-through-prayer.

9. For more about spreading God's love in your neighborhood, see the "Prayer-Care-Share" model (for example, on the Love2020 site, love2020.com/neighboring) and the "Learning a Pray-Care-Share Lifestyle" guide from WayMakers (waymakers.org/pray/prayer-care-share).

10. Dave Sanford, *Loving Your Neighbor: Surprise! It's Not What You Think* (CreateSpace, 2017), 253.

11. See the online resource guide for ideas about discovering and connecting the gifts of neighbors.

12. Linda Loosli, "Fifteen Ways to Get to Know Your Neighbors" (September 20, 2018), foodstoragemoms.com. See also Jacob Remes, "Finding Solidarity in Disaster," *The Atlantic* (September 1, 2015).

13. Marc Dunkelman, *The Vanishing Neighbor* (New York: Norton, 2014).

14. See, for example, Tracy Hadden Loh, Christopher Coes, and Becca Buthe, "Separate and Unequal: Persistent Residential Segregation Is Sustaining Racial and Economic Injustice in the U.S.," Brookings Institution (December 16, 2020); Antero Pietila, *Not in My Neighborhood: How Bigotry Shaped a Great American City* (Lanham, MD: Ivan R. Dee, 2010).

15. For example, Michelle Ferrigno Warren, *The Power of Proximity: Moving Beyond Awareness to Action* (Downers Grove, IL: IVP, 2017). See also Lynn Cory, *Neighborhood Initiative and the Love of God* (Colorado Springs, CO: NavPress, 2013).

16. Matthew Branaugh, "Know Your Neighbors?" *Christianity Today* (2012); Jay Pathak and Dave Runyon, *The Art of Neighboring: Building Genuine Relationships Right Outside Your Door* (Grand Rapids, MI: Baker Books, 2012).

8
You Were There for Me

Connect with People Who Are Isolated, Hidden, and Hurting

The Gospels are full of stories of Jesus making an intentional connection with people who were considered outsiders.

• Jesus stops in his tracks to call out to Zacchaeus, a despised tax collector, and invites himself over for dinner (Luke 19:1-10).

• When a woman with a stigmatized physical condition tries to remain inconspicuous while seeking healing, Jesus insists on personally meeting and encouraging her (Luke 8:43-48).

• People are shocked to see Jesus sitting and talking calmly with someone known to be demon-possessed, a man everyone feared and shunned (Luke 8:26-39).

• Jesus violates taboos to ask a favor from an outcast Samaritan woman, which leads to a deep, life-changing conversation (John 4:4-26).

This chapter explores how following Jesus can lead us to encourage and befriend people in contexts of isolation and struggle. This chapter is not primarily about meeting their physical and spiritual needs, though that too is vitally important.[1] Here our focus is on addressing the need for life-enriching personal connections.

Social isolation takes a significant toll on physical and mental health. Having regular contact with someone who cares about you can be literally life-giving. The church's vision can be that no one has to live in isolation or go through hard times alone. We envision a community in which everyone has someone who sees their value, enjoys their company, is with them in their struggles, and brings out their potential.

The Costs of Social Isolation
• Lacking social connections can be as damaging to health as smoking fifteen cigarettes a day.
• Loneliness raises the risk of early death by 30 percent (for seniors, 45 percent)
• Health effects of isolation among older adults costs around $6.7 billion annually in care
• Friendships reduce the likelihood of certain diseases and speed recovery for those who get ill.

Conclusion: "Few aspects of community are more powerful than the degree of connectedness and social support for individuals."[2]

Seeing Those Who Are Isolated, Hidden, and Hurting

The first step to making connections is learning to see people who are hidden and lonely—not just to identify their needs, but to be interested in them as whole persons. The pandemic amplified the crisis of social isolation already experienced by too many in our society. Those who face special barriers to connection include:

• people who are homebound due to age, disabilities, or medical conditions
• institutionalized populations such as residents of nursing homes, prisons, detention centers, or psychiatric hospitals
• people with isolating disorders like social anxiety, depression, or severe autism
• caretakers of a family member with a serious physical or mental health condition
• single parents with young children and no transportation
• residents in isolated rural areas
• undocumented immigrants

Being excluded and "invisible" often goes hand in hand with the sense of being devalued, of mattering less to others. "The consequence is a society in which poorer, older, and disabled Americans are kept systematically out of sight, out of mind."[3]

Pay attention to hidden pockets of loneliness. This could include individuals who lose their social circle after a divorce; LGBTQ+ youth lacking a supportive network; families that withdraw from social life to conceal a condition of addiction or abuse; or people who feel cut off from others after experiencing a tragic loss.

It may surprise people to know that young adults—especially young men—are the loneliest age group in America. In recent studies, two-thirds of young adults said that "no one really knows them well." Forty percent of young adults agreed with the statement, "I feel completely alone." Young adults also tend to feel they have less opportunity or confidence to make new connections.[4]

There are isolated, hidden, and hurting folks throughout your community—some probably in your neighborhood, or in your congregation. Perhaps that may even be how you describe yourself. A ministry leader who struggled with major depression during the pandemic urges everyone to look deeper:

> Some of you might say, I haven't run into someone suffering. The truth is, those of us that are usually don't like to broadcast it to the world. You've probably interacted with someone distressed and didn't know it. Even if you haven't, you will soon. Asking good questions to those around you can be very helpful. . . . "Are you doing okay right now?" or even "How are you REALLY doing right now?" A little question can go a long way with someone feeling alone. It communicates that you care.[5]

Cultivating Caring Connections

If you ask for it, God will bring someone in need of a supportive connection into your path. Perhaps you've been praying for someone in the congregation going through a difficult time and feel nudged by the Spirit to reach out in person, leading to a meaningful conversation. Perhaps you have been a volunteer for a caring ministry of the church or a nonprofit and want to get to know the people you have been serving. Perhaps you start noticing who may be lonely in your school, workplace, or neighborhood. Often, you have to be intentional about stepping outside your routine circle of connections to get to know someone with a life story quite different from your own.

As you connect with "hidden" people and learn their stories, prepare to have your perspective transformed. A church leader describes the shift that took place among volunteers as they began to make a personal connection with people in their housing ministry. "An awful lot of folks in this congregation, when we first started doing some of this stuff, said, 'I don't notice any poor people.' . . . Now not only do they see [them], but they hear the stories and they begin to become friends. And now, it's not just 'that poor bum on the street.' It's 'this guy I know.'"[6]

Shawna's Story

Shawna is case manager for Pathway of Hope, a Salvation Army program that helps families get out of a crisis. I (Heidi) asked her about the role that connections played in her own story of hardship.

My life used to be a mess. I even thought about hurting myself. I felt that if I died, no one would care. But then I found people who believed in me, and it changed my life.

Connections are like the frame that lifts you up. When you have people in your life who tell you that you matter, that you are good at something, it gives you a reason to get out of bed in the morning.

When I was struggling, I could count the number of supportive connections in my life on one hand; now I'd have to take my shoes off to count them all! I know people I can rely on if I need encouragement or advice. They give me confidence that I can figure things out.

After a difficult journey, I have a meaningful job helping other people. Now I'm the one reminding people that they matter and helping them find their purpose.

See chapter 3 for general pointers for starting a conversation; here we offer a few additional suggestions for cultivating connections focused on those who are hidden and hurting.[7] Connections may start with something as simple as learning someone's name, asking how their day is going, and listening to their response. It may lead to having regular conversations or doing things together. Sometimes—but not always—seeds of connection grow into that rare gift of a friend with whom you share life at a deeper level, in which each person finds their humanity affirmed and wholeness restored.

Eat together. As the story of Jesus and Zacchaeus illustrates, a meal is often a good place to begin a connection. What could this look like?

• Instead of serving the food at a local meal service program, accept a meal and eat beside others at the table.

• If a family who speaks little English moves into your neighborhood, learn enough of their language to invite them over for dessert.

• If you are out to eat and notice someone dining alone, introduce yourself and ask if they would enjoy company.

• Invite someone who has recently lost a spouse through death or divorce to your home for a meal on their birthday or a holiday.

I (Heidi) spent a lot of my school days eating alone and looking wistfully at the kids sitting in clusters. If someone had invited me to join their group—or came over with their friends to sit with me—I would have been slightly dazed, but overjoyed.

Invite stories. Story telling is a way of humanizing big social issues that can feel overwhelming. It can also build connections as you discover points you share in common. Some people are reluctant to share their story—perhaps because they have encountered judgment in the past. Others are open or even eager to let people know more about their life, and have amazing stories to tell. Informally, this can mean asking people questions that show you are curious about their life history and what it's like to walk in their shoes (see Questions to Invite Life Stories in Appendix

2). More formally, this might look like a listening project to collect and share life histories.[8]

Invite prayer. For some, it feels awkward to ask someone, "How can I pray for you?" Imagine saying instead, "I pray for three people every night before I go to bed. Would you like to be one of the three tonight? Is there anyone else you would like me to include in my prayer time? How can I pray for you?" Also consider inviting their prayers for you. "If you are a praying person, I would be grateful for prayer for my job, because it's hard right now."

Bring people together. A powerful way to foster connection is to bring people with similar life experiences together for mutual support. This may be as informal as introducing a teen mom to an older woman in your church who once also was a young single parent. It could look like hosting

---

Connecting with People with Disabilities
A few guidelines for communicating with courtesy and respect:[9]

1. Speak directly to a person with a disability, rather than to a companion or sign language interpreter who may be present. Don't use patronizing child-talk.

2. When talking with a person who has difficulty speaking, wait patiently for the person to finish, rather than correcting or speaking for them.

3. When speaking with a person in a wheelchair or using crutches, place yourself at eye level in front of the person. Do not lean on their wheelchair.

4. When speaking with someone who is hearing impaired, make sure they can see your mouth so they can read your lips, and do not shout.

5. Before jumping in to provide assistance (e.g., with opening doors), ask first and wait until the offer is accepted. If you're not sure how to help, ask.

The main thing to remember … How does a person with a disability want to be treated? Like a person! So, relax, and just be yourself.

---

a winter party for international students left on campus over break. Or it may mean launching an ongoing support group. (See suggestions for support groups in chapter 10.)

Serve a common cause. The most passionate advocates for a cause tend to be people who have had personal experiences with that issue. For example, if you want to connect with veterans, join an advocacy group working to improve health care for veterans. Working alongside people toward a shared goal is one of the best ways to start a meaningful relationship.

Being a Friend in Times of Struggle

It can be hard to be a friend to someone going through a tough time—illness or injury, financial struggles, family problems, loss. How do you connect in a meaningful way? As I (Heidi) reflect on the times when I leaned on my friends, I would say I am most grateful for three things: "You were there for me. You really listened to me. You helped my light shine." These phrases guide how we can seek to show support to others.

"You were there for me." The pastor of a church in a struggling neighborhood remarked, "The phrase that I hear when someone is grateful for support is this: 'You were there for me.' Not that you gave me this, or you did this for me—but 'You were *there* for me,' which means, 'You were there where I was, in whatever the situation was. . . . You had enough courage to be there for me and with me.'"[10]

"Being there" for and with people means showing up (in person or virtually), without judging. Make yourself available by asking, "How would you like me to be supportive?" Sometimes people want help processing a decision or dilemma, or they may need practical assistance, or just a kind gesture. People are often looking for compassionate companionship, someone willing to sit with them and just be there.

"You really listened to me." Hillary Doerries has long experience of building mutual support among people with mental health issues. She shares that when a person opens up to her, "I've learned to just let them talk, even if what they're saying is punctuated by moments of 'awkward' silence. My instinct is to fill in the silence with a response, or worse—ad-

vice." She has learned to respect these moments of "holy silence" as having a purpose: "to lean into their pain with your presence and not necessarily spoken words."[11]

It can be profoundly difficult to listen to someone share about a problem without jumping in to solve it. We naturally want to feel helpful, caring, and wise. Before saying anything, ask yourself: "Is this more about helping me feel better, or about being the good listener they need right now?"

As you listen to someone share their story, a similar experience you've had may come to mind. It can promote mutuality to disclose a time you also felt afraid, vulnerable, or alone—not in order to point out how you overcame it, but with the goal of invoking solidarity. However, saying "I know just what you are going through" may not be helpful, because it implies you don't need to keep listening. An empathetic response encourages further sharing: "I'm sad that happened to you. I've had to deal with something similar. Maybe sometime I can tell you about it."

"You helped my light shine." When someone is in a low spot, remind them how they are "fearfully and wonderfully made" (Psalm 139:14). What are their gifts? How do they bring joy to others? In what special way do they reflect God's glory (Matthew 5:16)?

What to Say When You Are Listening

If you catch yourself saying something like

You just need to . . . I think you should . . . What I would do is . . .
—this means you are probably more focused on solving their problem than on listening. Try saying something like this instead:

- "That sounds really hard."
- "What are you thinking about trying?"
- "Would you like to brainstorm some options together?"
- "I appreciate you sharing this with me."

See Appendix 2 for more questions to ask when you are being a supportive friend.

Help your friend shine by doing something that lights a spark of hope and joy. Take care of kids to give your friend restorative alone time. Do a life-enriching activity together: go on a nature walk, watch a sermon online, take an art class. Do a simple service project together—being a blessing to others may lead to feeling blessed.

Connections and Mental Health

People with mental health needs are at high risk of social isolation. "When the person isolates more, they face more mental distress. With more mental distress, they want to isolate. This vicious cycle relegates many people with severe mental illness to a life of social segregation and isolation."[12] Positive relationships can make a big difference, but there are some unique challenges to consider.

Many times, someone with mental illness is described as unreliable or a "bad friend" because they might cancel plans more

---

Be a Friend Who Helps in a Healthy Way

Friends naturally want to help one another. Proverbs 17:17 says, "A friend loves at all time." But this does *not* mean, "A friend is always available to help in every way." In a real connection, friends can be authentic about their limitations and feelings. The following red flags suggest a need to shift your relationship away from helping, toward a healthier connection:

- You feel guilty when you say no, but resentful when you say yes.
- You violate your boundaries to help them, telling yourself, "It's just this once."
- Your relationship centers on their struggles and your helping, with little mutuality.
- You are their only source of social support.
- Their problems are overwhelming and may require specialized assistance. (If your friend talks about hurting themselves or others, get help immediately: https://suicidepreventionlifeline.org/help-someone-else)

often than others. What you might not understand is the tremendous amount of energy it often takes to get through a normal day. Then add on top of that the effort to "go have fun" and that pressure can be too mentally exhausting. Set aside your judgement and don't give up on your friends. They are fighting a battle you will never fully understand.[13]

Four pointers for maintaining a friendship when mental health issues are in the picture:

1. Learn about the patterns associated with the specific mental health issues faced by your friend. This will help you not to take some behaviors personally, for example, if they do not return your messages.

2. Be flexible about plans, because a person's condition may suddenly change. Don't add guilt to their stress if they have to cancel.

3. Acknowledge that the pain that your friend may be experiencing is real, even if the source is not obvious to you. Don't pressure them to seek healing; accept that the struggle will be a part of the relationship. Bobbi Rose, a mental health advocate, shares, "Two of the worst things to say to someone with mental illness, or their family or caretakers, are 'You'll be fine!' and 'Don't worry.'"

4. Counter the stigma that accompanies mental illness with acceptance of your friend for who they are, as they are. Enjoy whatever the relationship has to offer in the moment.

Mental health issues are often intertwined with substance abuse, and the principles for maintaining supportive connections are similar.[14] For people in recovery, having a patient, knowledgeable, non-judgmental friend who affirms their God-given worth and purpose, even through the low times (without becoming enmeshed), can support their long recovery process. Be mindful too of maintaining connections with the family and caregivers of individuals struggling with addictions or mental illness, who may also be experiencing painful, stigmatizing isolation. Contact with friends, enjoying "normal life" kinds of activities together, renews hope and endurance for the long struggle.

Developing Trauma-Informed Connections

Becoming trauma-informed will enable you to nurture a wider range of connections with greater insight and compassion.

Trauma refers to a deeply distressing experience that causes physical or emotional damage. Childhood trauma such as abuse, neglect, violent loss, or family breakup can have long-lasting repercussions. For example, three-fourths of adults in substance abuse treatment report histories of abuse and other trauma.[15] Trauma and toxic stress put people at higher risk for physical and mental health problems. Because of these effects, trauma often reinforces social isolation.

A trauma-informed perspective helps to bridge this isolation. As you connect with people from contexts of hardship, it's important to develop a compassionate understanding of how toxic experiences may have affected them, and how this may show up in their relationships:

• They may have difficulty trusting people or forming new attachments. At the same time, their closest relationships may mean the world to them.

• They may appear to be hyper-sensitive and react with "fight, flight, or freeze"— a pattern of getting into conflicts, not showing up for things, or appearing to give up on a relationship.

• They may be fighting a hopeless, stuck feeling—that no matter how hard they try, life will slap them down again, so why bother?

• They are often people of deep faith who rely on God to make it through each day.

A trauma-informed way of building connections calls for the posture of mutuality, respect, and curiosity discussed in chapter 2. You may not be able to empathize fully with their experiences, but you can be open to learning more about what they have lived through and how this has shaped them. Be patient, mindful, and gracious in the process of building trust. Recognize that there may be bumps and barriers in the relationship that are not about you, but about the patterns of trauma in their past.

Trauma and resilience expert Rebecca Lewis-Pankratz explains,

> If we want to build connections to address isolation, our agenda can't be that we want to change people. Our goal is simply, "I want to know who you are and be connected with you." If we

Caden's Story: A Trauma-Informed Classroom Connection

At the ESSDACK Bridging to Resilience 2020 conference presentation on trauma-informed approaches to education, middle school teacher Megan Yoder introduced her former student, Caden,[17] as "brilliant, amazing and driven." This is his testimony (abridged).

I was twelve. I had a drug problem and was on probation. I was what some might call trouble. My first day at middle school was the worst. Since my reputation preceded me, all my teachers had formed opinions about me before they knew me. They treated me like I was a worthless criminal. It made me feel isolated and abandoned. But Ms. Yoder was awesome. Instead of ignoring me and putting me in a corner, she greeted me at the door, smiled at me, and made me feel welcome. Over the next few weeks she showed that she was truly there for me.

One day I got upset in math class, and I found myself going to Ms. Yoder's room. She talked with me, gave me a job to do in her classroom, gave me a snack, and helped me calm down. She always called me out when I knew I was doing something wrong. If I skipped a class, she pulled me aside to make up the missing work. Time and time again, she proved she wasn't going to give up on me. I'm in high school now and thriving because someone in seventh grade took a chance on me.

If I could give advice on how to handle a kid like me, it would be to show us respect. Be patient, because we've been through things you can't even imagine. You have the chance to make the biggest difference for someone like me. Show up, and be a Ms. Yoder for that kid.

show up just to build appreciative connection, transformation can happen. The way toward healing is by sharing stories and sharing our lives. These relationships enrich our lives deeply in ways we can't anticipate.[16]

Supportive, empowering, appreciative connections are a key to helping people develop resilience—the ability to return to being healthy and hopeful after bad things happen. Of course, other things are needed too, like health care and financial stability. But supportive relationships help all the other pieces come together. To overcome the toughest life challenges, you need people in your life that you can count on, who believe in you, who bring out the best in you, who share their time and pray faithfully for you. Becoming more trauma-informed helps us become that kind of friend.

From Isolation to Connection

I (Heidi) have a friend with a developmental disability who texts me almost every day: "Hi Heidi, how are you doing?" She is persistent in expecting a reply. If I don't answer right away, I might find a dozen messages waiting for me. Checking in to maintain our connection is important to us both.

Establishing rhythms of checking in regularly with others is part of what it takes to overcome isolation. It doesn't have to be complicated. Sending a "thinking of you, how are you doing today" message is a simple way for many of us to fit new connections into our busy lives. Being there for people is also expressed through the little things—like remembering their birthday or dropping off "just because" cookies—that say: *You matter to me, and I appreciate our connection.*

None of these ways of showing up for people are substitutes for professional help for individuals (such as counseling), social programs (such as senior centers), community development, and advocacy to address systemic problems. But it's also true that none of those things is a substitute for a real connection. "A sweet friendship refreshes the soul" (Proverbs 27:9, The Message).

Notes

1. Chapter 10 describes models for relationally oriented ministry in challenging contexts.

2. "The 'Loneliness Epidemic,'" U.S. Health Resources and Services Administration (January 17, 2019), www.hrsa.gov; Mylea Charvat, "The Impact of Social Isolation and Loneliness," *Psychology Today* (May 29, 2020), www.psychology-today.com.

3. David Hsu, *Untethered: A Primer on Social Isolation* (2018), 19.

4. "U.S. Loneliness Index," Cigna (2018); Jamie Ballard, "Millennials Are the Loneliest Generation," YouGov (July 30, 2019), https://today.yougov.com/topics/lifestyle/articles-reports/2019/07/30/loneliness-friendship-new-friends-poll-survey. See also Josh Packard and Ellen Koneck, *Belonging: Reconnecting America's Loneliest Generation* (Bloomington, MN: Springtide Research Institute, 2020).

5. Matt Svajda, "Another Pandemic Is Coming," Fiducia blog (May 5, 2020).

6. Quoted in Ronald J. Sider, Philip N. Olson, and Heidi Unruh, *Churches That Make a Difference: Reaching Your Community with Good News and Good*

If You Are Struggling and Lonely

If you recognize that you are struggling with isolation, or know someone in that situation, here are a few suggestions for reaching out.

Join a group. This could be a church small group, civic group, book club—anything that leads to regular interaction and opportunities for conversation.

Serve together. Look for volunteer opportunities that involve serving alongside others. For example, join the kitchen crew that prepares meals at a homeless shelter.

Pray together. At church, see who is talking about the same concern that you have, and invite them to get together with you to pray for this issue.

Share what you love to do. If you enjoy books, offer to read aloud to nursing home residents. If you enjoy woodworking, ask several youths to do a project with you.

Talk about connection. Speak out about wanting more meaningful connections in your life. It's a good bet that others feel the same way.

Get help if you need it. If you are struggling with thoughts of self-harm, call 800-273-8255 (Spanish: 888-628-9454). Visit www.mentalhealthfirstaid.org/2020/01/five-mental-health-resources-that-can-bet hedifference/ for additional mental health resources.

Works (Grand Rapids, MI: Baker Books, 2002), 92.

7. As in any context where you are forming personal connections, keep in mind the importance of maintaining safety guidelines and healthy boundaries (see Appendix 1).

8. When people trust you with their life stories, treat this as a precious gift, and remain respectful of people's dignity and privacy. If you plan to share someone's story publicly, get their approval first. Be wary of retelling stories in a way that reinforces negative stereotypes.

9. Adapted from "The Ten Commandments of Communicating with People with Disabilities" resource by United Cerebral Palsy Associates, and material provided by Erica Rivera, Executive Director, Prairie Independent Living Resource Center.

10. Quoted in Sider, Olson, and Unruh, *Churches That Make a Difference*, 90.

11. Comments shared in an email with the authors, December 17, 2020. See also Hillary's reflections on how her church supported her through a mental health crisis and "remained connected to me when I didn't feel like I was worthy of connection" in Hillary Doerries, "The Lord Has Done Great Things for Us, and We Are Glad Indeed: Loving and Serving Others Through Times of Mental Illness," UCC Mental Health Network (October 26, 2020).

12. Elise Stobbe, "Social Isolation and Mental Illness," BrainBlogger (May 15, 2006), https://brainblogger.com/2006/05/15/anti-stigmatization-social-isolation-and-mental-illness/.

13. Angela Howard, "How Mental Illness Affects Friendships" (August 9, 2020), https://hisheartfoundation.org/how-mental-illness-affects-friendships.

14. See McCarton Ackerman, "7 Tips for Being a Good Friend to Someone in Recovery," American Addiction Centers (December 18, 2019), www.recovery.org/7-tips-for-being-a-good-friend-to-someone-in-recovery.

15. Deena Mcmahon, "When Trauma Slips into Addiction," The Imprint (December 17, 2018), https://imprintnews.org/child-trauma-2/when-trauma-slips-into-addiction/32462.

16. Interview with Heidi Unruh on January 28, 2021.

17. Real names used with permission.

9
Difficult Conversations
How to Connect Across Deep Differences

One of the clear themes of the New Testament is early Christians running toward people everyone else is running away from. Again and again, God puts believers into settings where they are with people they have been told to avoid, and then God pushes them toward developing connection and community. The parable of the Good Samaritan (Luke 10:25-37)—breaking through social norms and stereotypes. Peter's vision of the clean and unclean—getting approval from God to minister to the Gentiles (Acts 10). And the new Christian churches—full of a diversity of people who weren't used to being together under any circumstances, much less for worship. There were a lot of bumps in the road along the way, as Paul so honestly described in his letters to the early churches.

The message is clear: Christians in the church are called into hard relationships, atypical for their time, that create a picture of hope, unity, and honest dialogue for the surrounding community. Maintaining these relationships requires us to have hard conversations.

After a particularly polarizing year, we wanted to write this chapter because we all feel divisions that can get in the way of the relationships that God is calling us to develop in the church and in our community. We invite you to consider having difficult conversations that feature listening with caring curiosity, with the goal of pursuing deeper connections.

The Purpose of Hard Conversations

This chapter provides guidance on how to have a one-on-one conversation with someone in your church or community with whom you have a substantive disagreement.[1] We call these "bridge-building conversations"—

dialogues that are difficult but necessary for maintaining connection across a difference. This process is recommended for use with someone you already know to a degree, not with a stranger.

We are not suggesting that you are responsible to work everything out with everyone you disagree with—or even that you have to like them. But failure to talk about hard things can be an impediment to life-giving relationships in the church and community. Not talking about the real issues when a conversation is needed can lead to hard hearts for the parties involved. We need to have open hearts toward each other for real connections to take root.

The goals of having these difficult conversations are:

- really listening to each other
- telling each other our stories, what lies behind our beliefs and values
- respecting one another's humanity regardless of disagreement
- reaching a new level of understanding and possibly acceptance of the other person

Bridge-building conversations are not about having a debate and declaring a "winner"; trying to change the other person's mind or recruit them for a cause; or resolving all our differences at once so we can completely clear the air of tension. These conversations start the process so that future dialogue is possible.

When Are Hard Conversations Needed?

Hard conversations can span any topic that generates division—from broad questions of theology and politics to specific concerns that are unique to your context. For example, people may be in conflict over the church's worship style, or how decisions in a ministry partnership get made.

Having a bridge-building conversation may be needed if:

- You find yourself avoiding someone at church or in the community because you have differing viewpoints or have had an argument.

• A relationship feels strained—you can't talk as easily as before, and you are not sure which topics are safe to discuss.

• Your congregation is dividing into factions because people don't agree on something that is important to them.

• You find yourself talking to others about your disagreement with a person but not to that person directly.

• You can't make progress on a significant issue because people with differing viewpoints don't understand each other and can't work together.

• Disagreements on certain issues are undermining a relationship that the church has developed with a community partner.

The aim is not to try to get every person in your church to agree on the issues of the day. On many issues, we can agree to disagree. Too often, however, agreeing to disagree means maintaining an angry silence. As Christians, we have to keep talking to one another.

The Challenge and Beauty of Bridge-Building Conversations

One of the problems with letting tensions "just slide," whether in the church or community, is that they tend to fester, growing worse over time. I (Joy) have worked in settings where unexpressed disagreements grew into factions, bitterness, and broken relationships, all of which affected the ability of the church to be the church to its members and in the community. Stepping forward to have these conversations takes courage, but the reality is that if you don't dialogue, things are likely to get much worse.

We might avoid a hard conversation with someone because we are afraid we might hurt their feelings and damage the relationship. However, these conversations can end up strengthening the relationship. Taking the risk involved demonstrates a level of commitment and courage that lets the person you are talking with know that you care. This can also inspire other people to have hard bridge-building conversations too.

Don't let fear be what holds you back. What I (Heidi) regret the most is the relationships that have drifted away quietly because I was afraid to have a conversation.

Having fruitful bridge-building conversations can create openings for new ministry and new ways of seeing God working. Taking the step forward to talk constructively is a spiritual act that can soften our hearts and make us more receptive to what God is trying to do in us and through the ministry of our church.

Another benefit of a hard conversation is that it can help keep your mind open about the characteristics and motivations of those "other people" you disagree with. It can be easy to stereotype everyone who holds a particular viewpoint as being a certain way. When you talk to someone in that group, though, you realize that people have a variety of complex reasons for the views they hold. You come to view them as a unique individual, not a caricature.[2]

You can also learn about yourself in powerful ways through difficult conversations. You may learn more about your biases, how strongly you hold certain viewpoints and why, what motivates you and makes you angry. You may learn something painfully true about yourself that needs to change—cynicism or negativity about something or someone, for example.

There are issues in our communities that we can make progress on only if we are willing to have difficult conversations. People who are different in a number of ways will need to come together with all of their gifts and passion to address environmental issues, hunger, affordable housing, access to health care, and the list goes on. Having these conversations opens us up to the possibility that everyone has assets to bring to the table, even if we don't agree with them on everything.

Finally, having bridge-building conversations affirms that we are created for relationships. We can disagree passionately, and yet remain connected. This gives us a better appreciation for Jesus as the reconciler of all things (2 Corinthians 5:18).

Get Yourself Ready for a Difficult Conversation

There is some work you should do to prepare, to make sure you are ready for a conversation like this, and it doesn't involve practicing your arguments or having the best retorts. I (Joy) confess I have tried it that way a few times, without much success. These steps are more about your perspective and the condition of your heart going into a conversation. Think and pray through these steps.[3]

Spend time in prayer. Pray for the other person, that God would prepare their heart for the conversation and allow them to be honest and open. Then pray the same thing for yourself. Pray that the conversation would be fruitful and that it would strengthen your relationship.

Give up the need to change the other person. The purpose of these conversations is not to get the other person to change their mind and concede you are right. The goal is to communicate with each other even through our differences—to listen and more fully understand the beliefs of the other person and why they hold them.

Let go of the need to advance an agenda. Perhaps you are personally committed to forward movement on a larger issue, whether that involves politics, justice or theology, or progress on something you would like to see happen at your church. The purpose of this conversation is not to recruit another person to your cause, which would shift the conversation to trying to convince the other person to take a position or make a commitment. Here, your job is to listen.

Be aware of your emotions. Conflict brings with it a maelstrom of emotions, which you can't remove from the conversation—nor should you try. They are a part of you. The more you are aware of your own feelings, the more empathy and understanding you can show to the other person regarding their emotions. Prepare by reflecting (in your journal, or to a trusted friend):

- The main emotions that this topic brings up in me are . . .
- The main emotions that I'm feeling toward the other person are . . .
- How do I expect to express my emotions in our conversation?
- How do I hope to feel at the end of our conversation?

Discover your own biases. Everyone stereotypes or prejudges others in some way. Our biases stem from a variety of sources, some deeply embedded in our subconscious from our upbringing or context. While facing this may be complex and painful, it's important to do the work of uncovering your biases.[4] Even seemingly trivial predispositions can still be real barriers to mutual relationship.

In preparing for hard conversations, we are not aiming to declare, "I am completely bias-free." The goal is to be more aware of our biases so we can be alert for them in our interactions. If we acknowledge our stereotypes, we can consciously choose to reject them as we are having our conversation, and instead regard the other person with respect.

Have an openness to being surprised or enlightened. We described openness as a quality that is important to deep connections in chapter 2, and you will definitely need it in difficult conversations. You may think you know all about the person you are talking to and what is behind their viewpoint, but prepare to be surprised.

- Be open to learning something unexpected about the other person.
- Be open to seeing an issue from a different perspective—one you had not thought of before.
- Be open to seeing errors in your own viewpoint. Pray for humility: "Have the mindset that you might not be right. Be open to discovering new possibilities together."[5]
- Be open to seeing where you need to grow—for example, being willing to get more information before making a snap judgment.
- Be open to viewing the other person as someone who is not your enemy.

Be open to the work of the Holy Spirit. Ask God for eyes to see the other person with new appreciation, ears to hear what they are saying, and a heart that can understand. Be sensitive to the Spirit's leading. You may start out with prepared questions (for example, see the Questions to Explore Someone's Perspective in Appendix 2), or an idea about how things are going to go, but the Spirit may lead you in a different direction that results in greater connection. So be prepared for what God will do because you have taken the courageous step forward to have the conversation.

Starting the Conversation

How would you initiate a bridge-building conversation with someone?

A clear invitation. A direct approach is probably the best way to invite someone into the conversation, with clarity about the purpose. You might say something like, "I think we have different opinions on the issue of immigration, and I would like to sit down and have a conversation with you on that topic. I am interested in hearing about your viewpoints and understanding where you are coming from on this. I would also like to share my viewpoints and why I hold them."

Then explain that this is not an argument or a debate; the goal is not to change each other; the emphasis is on listening for understanding; and you want to have the conversation in order to deepen your connection with them, not to damage it.

Set ground rules for the conversation. We recommend agreeing to a set of basic ground rules with the other person before you start. These guidelines help the conversation stay focused on the goal of strengthening your relationship through mutual understanding and learning.

• Ask each other, "What do you need to feel safe in this conversation?"

• Agree not to have a debate—going back and forth with facts and ideas until one person "wins" over the other person. It can be difficult not to slip into debate mode. There are a number of strategies you could try: allowing each person to talk uninterrupted for a set time (up to five minutes); having the rule that each person can ask clarifying questions but is not allowed to make counterstatements; using an object like a talking stick; having a third party present to help the conversation stay within bounds. Experiment with the guidelines and accountability that work for you.

• Agree that the other person is the expert on their own story. This means I can't say your description of your experiences is incorrect, or tell you how you should feel.

• Commit to confidentiality—neither of you will share what is said in this conversation with other people, except by mutual consent.

• Commit to respectful communication—reserving judgment, avoiding labeling, using respectful terms.

• Have a plan in advance for handling offended or hurt feelings, which are likely to occur. One strategy is to use the terms "yellow zone" when you are coming up to your line of painful feelings, and "red zone" to express that you are not okay and may need to step back. For example: "I have had hurtful experiences around that label, and I am getting into a yellow zone. Can we talk about this in a different way?"

• Indicate whether you are open to constructive critique, by saying something like: "I'm still learning how to say things in a constructive way. If you want to share anything about how I could be more respectful in my comments, that would help me out."

Tips for Having a Hard Conversation That Is Fruitful

Start by expressing appreciation to one another for agreeing to take part in the dialogue and reaffirm the importance of your relationship.

Practice undivided and deep listening. This will require you to set aside some time (about an hour) and to be in a space where you won't be interrupted. Stay off the phone or computer and just sit and listen. Active listening practices especially important for bridge-building conversations include:

• giving your partner your full attention and waiting until they are finished speaking before you respond

• reflecting what your partner is saying to you—periodically paraphrasing what they've said

• asking questions to clarify something you don't understand

• summarizing—restating major themes as the conversation proceeds[6]

Practice honest sharing. While your primary goal is to listen and grow in understanding, you are also sharing your own perspective. Otherwise this would be an interview, not a dialogue. Don't monopolize, but communicate as candidly and clearly as you can. Take ownership of your opinions and feelings by using "I" statements (*I believe, I think, I feel . . .*), whenever you catch yourself using "you" statements (*you are, you don't, you shouldn't* . . .).

Find commonalities. Do enough conversing at the beginning to find some commonalities—things both of you may be involved in at church or in the community. This can set a positive tone for the conversation.

Encourage telling your stories. A good starting point for the meat of the conversation is to explore one another's personal background in relation to the topic under consideration. Get people talking about their life experiences. This helps to keep the topic grounded in who you both are as individuals, rather than abstract arguments. Questions to explore background context include:

- When did this topic become important to you?
- Who in your life has influenced you or helped you shape your views?
- Have your views changed over the years? If so, why?
- What experiences have you had in relation to this topic?

As you share about your lives, look for other points of commonality that may emerge.

Focus on vision. Discussions tend to remain more positive when they focus not on the current problem but on your vision for the future. Even when a person is "against" something, they can (with encouragement) trace it to the positive outcomes they believe would result from ending that "something."

Try using "What do you wish . . ." questions:

- What do you wish would happen in our community that isn't happening now?
- How do you wish the issue we are talking about could be resolved?
- What's your vision for how this could play out in the future—what do you wish would result if your perspective on this issue came to pass?

Get at the belief behind the belief. Ask questions about how the other person came to their views—the reasoning behind it, why the issue is important to them, how their views may have changed over the years. As noted in chapter 3, asking "why" directly about sensitive topics can put people on the defensive, so frame questions in a way that comes across as curious rather than combative.

- What makes this issue important to you?
- What core values are you trying to protect? Underlying values often reflect elemental needs—safety, freedom, respect, belonging.
- How does your faith come in as you relate to this topic?
- What has influenced your view on this subject? This might include cultural background or personal history, a person or a philosophy, or teachings of Scripture or the church.

Look for shared values. Try to spot the values you share, even if you have very different beliefs about how those values get expressed and addressed. For example, maybe both of you care about hungry people being fed, but one of you thinks that the government should take more responsibility for this, and the other thinks it should be addressed through private efforts. Getting to a point of seeing a common goal is a breakthrough, even if you still advocate different ways to get there. If you discover what both of you are passionate about, keep that in front of you as you talk.

When you feel critical, get curious. As we have described throughout the book, curiosity is a powerful tool in developing real connections. If you begin to feel judgmental during the conversation, ask more open-ended questions to move toward deeper understanding and empathy. Get at the "whys" and encourage story telling.

One option is to ask some "I wonder" questions:

- I wonder what makes you so passionate about this?
- I wonder what challenges you have faced in relation to this issue?
- I wonder what makes people get so angry about this issue?

• I wonder what you think I don't understand yet?

Get curious about yourself as well! See When It's Hard to Listen in Appendix 2. Ask yourself questions like:

• I wonder why that statement made me feel so upset?
• I wonder how I got to that conclusion?
• What is my goal in the conversation right now?

Model care and self-care. If you sense that the heat is rising, pause for a check on the relationship by asking one another:

• How are you doing right now?
• Would it be helpful to reaffirm of our purpose and ground rules?

When Not to Engage

Generally, we can expect that difficult conversations will have rough patches that require us to be thick-skinned and forgiving. However, if the conversation gets too difficult, then for the sake of your well-being and the relationship, you will need to walk away.

We recommend you end the conversation if:

• the other person is clearly at the table to convert you to their view, not to dialogue in order to strengthen a connection with you
• it's clear the other person is disinterested in having a dialogue and talks over you and repeats their views
• there are personal attacks, name calling, or labeling
• the person you are talking with is acting angry, yelling, bullying, or being abusive and disruptive in other ways
• you are getting so angry that you stop seeing the other person as a human being

If this happens, you may need to get help from a third party to bring healing in the relationship.

• Do we need a break, or do we choose to keep going?

• Is there anything you need from me? (Is there anything I need to do to take care of myself?)

Keep connection at the center. When the conversation gets frustrating or uncomfortable, remind yourself of your purpose—to pursue God's plan for bridge-building relationships. Re-centering on the relationship may refresh your commitment to the conversation.

Bring closure. When you reach the end of your appointed time frame or a good stopping point, express affirmations of what you've learned and an appreciation for the other person's willingness to talk. You may each wish to share one thing you understand better about the other person as a result of the conversation. Then decide if you want to talk again.

Considerations for Hard Conversations Involving Race

Although this chapter is not focused on racial dialogues, issues of race will enter into many hard conversations. Consider these unique concerns.

Talk, but don't just talk. A conversation like this is not a substitute for the ongoing hard work of taking action to confront racism.

Educate yourselves. To learn more about racism, particularly systemic issues, do not use difficult conversations for the purpose of educating yourself. Read books, connect with community organizations that provide training, and attend events that will provide you with information and perspective. Bridge-building conversations as we have laid out here are for hearing each other and deepening relationships, not for filling in gaps in knowledge.

Difficult conversations about race need to be grounded in a relationship. There are some issues you can discuss fruitfully with someone you have only a casual connection with—but race is not one of them. The process we have laid out here is best when there is already some history of a connection and a degree of mutual trust.

When urgent action is needed, show up. There are critical times when you or your congregation should show up to respond, perhaps before you have had conversations about race. If there is white supremacist activity in your community, for example, you should stand against it now, not just schedule a conversation.

Keep Talking

I (Joy) realized in recent years that I have learned most of what I know about difficult conversations by being a mother to two teens during their middle school and high school years. We have had many disagreements and differing philosophical views, but I always said to my kids that the goal was to keep talking. We weren't going to break our relationships over differing viewpoints. The point was to stay in relationship and keep talking in order to understand each other better and maintain our connection.

We encourage you to keep talking to one another, by having difficult conversations—so that you can strengthen your relationships, grow in mutual understanding, and come together to do the work of the church.

Notes

1. This chapter does not address group dialogue or community-wide conversations, though that can also be a constructive step in building connections across divisions. Note also that the method we outline here is designed to address divisions involving beliefs or viewpoints, not personal grievances. If someone expresses views about women in leadership that I disagree with, that might call for a conversation; but if someone has made hurtful sexist remarks directed toward me personally, that calls for different resolution tools.

2. Oriented to Love is a great example of a ministry that breaks down stereotypes and walls to build unity among diverse Christians. One of the ways Oriented to Love does this is through retreats that bring together LGBTQ and straight/cisgender Christians for group dialogues across deep difference, with a commitment to mutual vulnerability and respect. For more about the program, see: www.christiansforsocialaction.org/programs/oriented-to-love/.

3. Also prepare by reviewing the references for difficult bridge-building conversations in the online resource guide.

4. The Teaching Tolerance resource kit from the Southern Poverty Law Center has a good summary of what hidden biases are, their impact, and how they can be combatted, plus information on Implicit Association Tests (IAT). See www.tolerance.org/professional-development/test-yourself-for-hidden-bias.

5. Ed O'Malley and Amanda Cebula, *Your Leadership Edge* (Wichita, KS: Kansas Leadership Center Press, 2015), 120.

6. See references on active listening in the online resource guide.

10
Models for Relational Ministry
Programs That Focus on Building
Supportive Relationships

We have emphasized so far that churches need to create space for relationships to develop organically. At the same time, programs can be a great way for a church to cultivate more connections. Think of programs as hospitality—setting out an invitation and welcoming table. You can't program relationships, but you can create intentional space where they may take root and grow.

In this chapter we look at a range of models for programs that have an intentional component of building relationships. What these varied models have in common is that connectedness is not just a means to an end but part of the desired outcome. This sampling of programs lays out some of the possibilities for what might be helpful in your context.[1] In choosing a program model, you should always start with listening to determine what the community says it most needs and wants, as well as listening in your congregation to see what might be a good fit (see the online listening guide).

We will look at examples of program models in four areas: supportive relationships within the church; bridging church members and people in the community; connections with special groups; and empowering relationships to walk with people with complex needs.

Program Models for Connection within the Congregation
Chapter 4 shared ideas for congregations wanting greater connectedness, including various kinds of small groups. Here are a few other examples of programs that create structured opportunities for church members to form deeper relationships.

Intergenerational mentoring relationships match a youth with an adult in the church who offers special attention and caring guidance. At Heidi's congregation, First Mennonite Church, this is called "Mentor & Mentee"—M&M for short. Monthly meetings feature a meal (with M&Ms for dessert, of course), one-on-one discussion questions, and then a group activity. My kids' mentors remembered their birthdays, came to school events, and found other ways to show interest in their lives. (All adults had to go through safety training and be approved.)

Stephen Ministry provides one-to-one care for individuals in the congregation going through difficult situations like divorce, job loss, serious illness, or death of a loved one. A trained Stephen Minister meets weekly with the person to develop a caring relationship, for as long as it is needed. Their primary role is to "listen, care, encourage, and provide emotional and spiritual support" (www.stephenministries.org). BeFriender Ministry (www.befrienderministry.org) is a similar model.

Program Models for Bridging Church and Community

Chapter 6 addressed the important goal of making connections with the broader community. One way to do this is through programs in which people "inside" and "outside" the church can interact socially.

Sports and exercise programs for children or adults can include exercise classes, active living groups (like a running club), and sports leagues. Programs may be set in a church gym or held in partnership with a local YMCA or fitness center. Coaches often develop close mentoring relationships with youth and may also encourage them in their faith.

Various types of art groups create a space for "creatives" to gather for making, discussing, and enjoying art. It could start with a group of artists at your church who invite in other local artists. The group could meet at a studio or in a room in the church building equipped as a workspace and stocked with supplies. The format could include classes, discussion, and work time. This could work well with intergenerational groups and could also include dance, theater, music, and other art forms.

A variation on this might involve a "makerspace" or robotics center where groups of more technologically-oriented creatives can interact.

Community discussion groups set the table (literally) for dialogues about topics of interest, from immigration to parenting to disappointment with God. Everyone's perspective is welcome. Usually the format includes food, a presentation, and conversation starters for table groups to discuss, in a relaxed atmosphere. Those sitting around a table together, ideally a mix of church members and community residents can get to know one another on equal footing. While a faith-based perspective may be explored, the goal in this setting is not to teach but to encourage

Forming a Missional Community

Grace Gathering in Fort Wayne, Indiana, helps people form missional communities called a "family on mission," which they define as "a group of people who seek to know God's love, treat each other as family, and pursue people together with God's love."

One family on mission at Grace is a group of teen guys who built on their friendship to form a core team. A team member describes their connectedness: "We pray in the morning every day before school. We hang out together on the weekends. We're very involved in each other's lives."

Their sense of mission leads them to be attentive to other students who may be lonely or hurting. "One day at lunch we saw this kid sitting alone, and we felt called to go sit with him. We talked with him and got to know him a little bit. The next day we went and sat with him again. We try to continually bring people into our lives and make them feel accepted and be a part of our family."

The boys invite other teens to hang out with their core team and to participate in the church's weekly youth group. They have seen their "family" grow as youth have joined the group, embraced Christian faith, and asked to be baptized—then started inviting others.

Adapted from the story shared at www.gracegathering.com/stories /driven-a-youth-family-on-mission

participants to share their questions, thoughts, and life experiences relevant to the topic.[2]

Missional communities are small groups of church members dedicated to two goals: building authentic relationships with one another and reaching out to connect with people outside the church. Any group in the church can develop a missional identity by shifting its focus outward. For example, a college group might be intentional about building a network of relationships in the gamer community.

Support groups connect people facing similar life situations, regardless of whether they are church attenders. The freedom to be open about their struggles—such as losing a spouse, facing a serious illness, or having a family member with an addiction—can create a unique bond. GriefShare (griefshare.org), DivorceCare (divorcecare.org), and Celebrate Recovery (celebraterecovery.com) are examples of established support group models found in many churches.

Connect through a Mental Health Support Group

Music minister Hillary Doerries shares the story of her first experience with a mental health support group. As she listened to people share their raw stories, she recalls the deeply moving feeling that she had "found my people": "This is the beauty of a support group . . . when an individual is empowered to share her innermost thoughts and struggles in a room filled with other people who understand and empathize. . . . Somehow, a small space inside of us begins to soften and slowly open."[3]

Later, after joining the staff at Christ the King Lutheran Church in South Bend, Indiana, Hillary helped launch a group called Fresh Hope for Mental Health at the church, so others could come together toward healing. The church also sponsors a grief group.

Pastor Caroline Satre explains how modeling "authentic vulnerability" is key to their church's ministry culture that helps these groups thrive. "We believe in honestly sharing our own joys and struggles and making space for others to do the same. This isn't weakness; it's brave. It's godly. It's community-forming."

"Third space" ministries provide space and hospitality where people can hang out and build connections, often along with some targeted activities. This can take many forms: coffee house, drop-in center, senior center, play area, community room. In small towns lacking public spaces, this can be a particularly vital service.

A thrift store sponsored by a group of churches observed a need among its customers for family-friendly opportunities to socialize. The We Care Community Center was launched, with the churches (including Heidi's church) facilitating the gathering one evening a week. "We wanted a place for people to feel safe and accepted and supported, to share a meal, play games and just hang out," says organizer Jane Wagler. "There's no judgment, no requirements. It's just a place to be together."[4]

Program Models for Connecting with Special Groups

The program models below illustrate how church members can cultivate connections with a particular demographic group. (Another recommended strategy is to partner with a community organization connected with that demographic group—see chapter 6.)

Connect with kids. For churches that are new to relational community ministry, engaging with children may be a good starting place: kids are easy to find, a natural bridge from the congregation into the community—and they're fun. There are a plethora of program models for engaging children from both the church and the community. A relational approach to ministry with children (or teens) means that the main agenda is building the connection, regardless of what activity you are doing. Make sure that any children's program complies with safety guidelines for interacting with youth (see Appendix 1).

One common option is to partner with a local elementary school. Work with school staff to find the best way to connect with students, whether tutoring, lunch buddies, after-school program, or helping kids tend a school garden. Kids Hope USA (kidshopeusa.org) offers a simple, proven program model.

Connect with teens. There are a wide range of program models for building meaningful connections with youth in the community, including:

• Teen hangout—provide a safe and cozy place for youth to come after school and do homework, play online, learn life skills like healthy cooking, and other fun or enriching activities, with the supervision and companionship of church members.

• Job shadowing—help youth develop their career interest and then match them with a role model in this field, to bring them to work and talk with them about their career path.

• Entrepreneurship—engage teens in developing a small business idea (e.g., selling snacks or doing yardwork), with an enthusiastic adult mentor supporting them from start to finish.

• Challenge clubs—provide a group of youth with equipment, training, regular practice times, devotions, and confidence-building coaching to reach a big goal (long run, big hike, step dance performance).

Connect with young adults. Research suggests that two out of three young church attenders become disconnected from church life in the years

Rites of Passage

Trinity Missionary Baptist Church in Gary, Indiana, has a mission of empowering youth. One important way this is expressed is through their rites of passage groups, equipping teens with life skills and self-confidence. Their God's Girls Rock group, for example, hosted activities such as a seminar on finances, and a panel of women sharing about their career paths. The Lifting as We Rise mentoring program has graduated more than one hundred young men since its launch in 2005.

In a city with high unemployment, the program gives youth a hiring advantage. Pastor Dwight Gardner explains, "We created jobs for a number of young men in the summer who are spending three days a week doing work for senior citizens and the community, such as cleaning out garages, mowing lawns and fence painting, to help build and teach that work ethic" (quoted in *Jet*, August 4, 2008, 47).

following high school graduation.[5] This age group also tends to be skeptical of church programs that seem patronizing or inauthentic. Suggested program areas involve forming community around the arts; activism; adulting (e.g., finances or car maintenance); networking for employment; and making meals.

St. Mark's Episcopal Church in Philadelphia, PA, sponsors a program called "Rise," which twice a month leads a group through the process of making bread from scratch. While the dough is rising, a facilitator from the church leads the group in conversations about social justice issues, such as human rights. After enjoying fresh bread, the group delivers some of the loaves to nearby food pantries. One advantage of this program for building relationships: "Bread has to rise for an hour. So, they have a captive audience."[6]

International Women's Book Club

The mission of Knoxville International Network (KIN) is that "Internationals are welcomed as neighbors, embraced as family, and enjoy lives of hope, dignity, and purpose in Christ Jesus." KIN helps churches develop relational outreach to welcome and befriend people from other countries. This is one such story.[8]

Growing up overseas, Laura had been the foreigner, understanding neither the language nor the culture. So as an adult, when her church connected with a nearby apartment complex, Laura quickly understood that God wanted her to carve time out of her schedule for the international women—mostly refugees—who live there.

Now, Laura leads a book club before the formal ESL class; then she watches the young children while their mothers attend class. She's been working at this apartment complex for two years. It has taken that long for the women to trust her enough to invite her into their homes, to visit her home, and to ask more personal questions about the cultural issues they face.

That means the book club doesn't always get around to discussing the book, but that's OK with Laura—because the relationships are more important than the program.

Connect with people new to this country. Chapter 5 gave ideas for congregations seeking a multicultural church partnership. Other suggestions:[7]

• Family-to-Family: Form a pod that matches two American-born families with two international families and organize monthly potluck meals and kid-friendly events.
• Culture Clubs: Take a group of people new to this country and American-born church members together to experience events or sites with cultural significance (concert, museum, Fourth of July parade).
• Invite international students to serve alongside church members in your church's volunteer projects in the community.

Connect with people with disabilities. Develop programs that build relationships around the gifts and interests of people with disabilities.

Friendship House

Mount Pleasant United Methodist Church helped to launch Terre Haute Friendship House, which provides affordable housing for up to eight college students and young adults with disabilities ("Friend Residents"). More than just a place to live, the house fosters mutual community. Church members often come over to cook meals with the residents and eat together.

Residents have also had an impact on the church. Jess Berryhill, Special Needs Ministry Coordinator at Mt. Pleasant, says these connections are helping church members see their neighbors with disabilities—and God—in a new way: Friendship House residents have served our congregation communion, participated in advent readings, and found teams to serve on each week. Our residents have become totally immersed in our church's culture and they are changing the way our church sees disability. Friendship House has reignited opportunities to have conversations about inclusion in our church."[9]

Walking with People with Complex Needs

Empowering, supportive relationships are at the core of a number of program models that help people get through a crisis or overcome deep-seated challenges, often coming out of a context of trauma. This approach might be called "walking with" ministry. It typically entails a longer-term commitment (six to eighteen months) to connect with someone as they work toward their goals for a better life, staying with them through the ups and downs of a transformative journey.

Circles (circlesusa.org). Circles trains and supports people to break the hold of entrenched poverty. Rachel, a graduate of Circles of Hope Reno County at Trinity United Methodist Church in Hutchinson, KS, now works for a program to promote resilience. She describes the significance of empowering relationships:

> In Circles you don't have to do it on your own. You are matched with two people called Allies. You eat together, talk regularly, and invest in each other. They become an anchor for you, walking alongside you as you make all these changes. They encourage you, have compassion for you, and help you learn to advocate for yourself.

Beth, one of the two Allies who walked with Rachel, says she too was transformed by the experience. "Conversation, encouragement and learning together over time are powerful tools of hope for change. Sharing this with Rachel has gifted me with a holy friendship."

Bridge of Hope (bridgeofhopeinc.org). This initiative connects single mothers experiencing homelessness with a team of six to eight "Neighboring Volunteers" from a local congregation, along with a case manager and targeted financial assistance. "Loneliness and isolation is so real for families facing homelessness," says Bridge of Hope CEO Edith Yoder. The bridge in this program is not only out of homelessness but also into caring community.

Prison re-entry programs. After incarceration, former offenders face a host of barriers to reintegrating into the community. Greater Warner

Tabernacle A.M.E. Zion Church in Knoxville, TN builds "relational equity" with former offenders, offering advocacy and encouragement as they find jobs, housing, and a better path forward. They also host "The Round Table," a weekly dialogue for ex-offenders and their families to discuss their concerns in a setting of love, support, and understanding (connectministries.net).

Youth mentoring. A consistent, caring adult relationship is one of the most important factors in helping youth to overcome disadvantage or trauma, and to have a wider range of future options.[10] Many community-based mentoring programs rely on volunteers from churches. For example, Amachi (amachimentoring.org) matches nurturing adults with children who have an incarcerated parent.[11] YouThrive (youthrive.org) trains a Support Family to help older teens who are transitioning out of foster care. If a church is interested in starting its own mentoring program, www.mentoring.org provides practical details.[12]

Relationships Provide a Bridge to Housing and Hope

Sheri remembers the first time her church's Bridge of Hope team met Jayden [name changed], a young single mother trying to find a stable place to live. "It felt awkward—we were all asking her questions, trying to get to know her." But over the next twelve months, the relationship grew through day-to-day acts of companionship: text messages, meeting for coffee, walks in the park. Jayden's new friends stood by her through an unanticipated job loss, a crash that totaled her car, and her son's medical needs. There were celebrations, too, marking Jayden's new career as a certified nurse aide—and a regular paycheck.

Financial assistance got Jayden into a home, but having friends helped her secure a future.

Keys for Relationships in "Walking with" Programs

The relational values we laid out in chapter 2—being a great listener, curious, respectful, asset-minded, available, and open—are vital to the success of a "walking with" ministry program. As a mentor, sponsor, or other support role, the following principles will help you engage constructively with someone who is seeking a better life.

Respect them as your equal. View each individual (no matter their situation) with appreciation as God's unique and gifted creation. It's OK (in fact, it's inevitable) to disagree with someone or even to be disappointed in them . . . but never condescend.

Don't try to be their savior. (Jesus is enough!) Sometimes Christians serve people out of the misguided attitude that we have been sent to rescue them on God's behalf. But this savior posture stands in the way of genuine connection. A person can't be our project *and* our friend.

Earn their trust. Be patient, and don't be offended if people keep you at arm's length until you show you are trustworthy. If they open up to you, avoid responding with lecturing, advice, judging or freaking out—or by repeating it to others (even as a prayer request).

Do things with people, not for them. Don't assume that when someone tells you about a problem, it means that they want you to fix it for them. Ask, "What do you need from me in this situation?" What they want most may be your listening ear, support for their problem solving, and encouragement that they can take the next step. (See the set of questions for helping someone make progress toward a goal in Appendix 2.)

Enjoy a mutual relationship. Focus on people's gifts and potential, not just their problems and needs. Be open to learning and receiving from the person you support. Focus on what you like about the other person, and don't be afraid of "wasting time" by having fun.

If your church is considering any type of "walking with" ministry program, we recommend training volunteers in these key principles, as well as boundaries and safety guidelines (see Appendix 1). It can also be helpful to introduce volunteers to trauma-informed ministry practices.[13]

"Walking with" programs tends to be mutually transformative. As a relational ministry leads to greater awareness and empathy for people's struggles, don't be surprised if your church is moved to want to learn more and take action on issues you perhaps never considered before. Real connections can be a catalyst for a renewed calling to "act justly and to love mercy" (Micah 6:8).

We're All Just People

When I (Heidi) was in college, I volunteered to lead my church's Vacation Bible School with kids who lived ina public housing complex. Before my first site visit I worked myself up to an anxious dither. What was the best way to introduce myself? How should I relate to families who lived in poverty or came from different cultures? What if I talked too much or too little? What if I accidentally offended someone?

Finally my mother intervened: "Good grief, Heidi, relax. We're all just people." It's still good advice.

C. S. Lewis made a similar point, but with a little more fanfare: "There are no ordinary people. You have never talked to a mere mortal. Next to the Blessed Sacrament itself, your neighbor is the holiest object presented to your senses" (*The Weight of Glory*).

We humans can be prideful, destructive, maddeningly foolish, and horrifically selfish. But never forget for a moment that God created people to be awesome and to live connected with other people in a way that brings out our awesomeness. That's what it means to be "just people." In whatever form it takes, whether focused on the congregation or engaged with the community, the essence of a great relational program is that it is a faithful reflection of that design.

Notes

1. Additional program descriptions can be found in Joy Skjegstad, *7 Creative Models for Community Ministry* (Valley Forge, PA: Judson Press, 2013) and Ronald J. Sider, Philip N. Olson, and Heidi Unruh, *Churches That Make a Difference: Reaching Your Community with Good News and Good Works* (Grand Rapids, MI: .Baker Books, 2002). While we don't discuss evangelistic programs specifically in this chapter, it is our hope that any of the models we describe present opportunities for sharing God's love in word and deed.

2. One resource for this model is Lifetree Café (lifetreecafe.com). Alpha (alphausa.org) is another resource specifically for those looking for a more evangelistic focus to the discussions.

3. Hillary Doerries shared her story on the website for Christ the King Lutheran Church, www.ctkluth.com/freshhope.html.

4. John Green, "Hutchinson Center Offering Free Monday Night Fellowship and Meal," *The Hutchinson News* (March 12, 2019), www.hutchnews.

com/news/20190312/hutchinson-center-offering-free-monday-night-fellowship-and-meal.

5. "Most Teenagers Drop Out of Church as Young Adults," Lifeway Research (January 15, 2019), https://lifewayresearch.com/2019/01/15/most-teenagers-drop-out-of-church-as-young-adults.

6. Grace Maiorano, "Historic Bella Vista Church Hosts Baking Bread Sessions to Spur Social Change," *South Philly Review* (October 14, 2019), https://south-phillyreview.com/2019/10/14/historic-bella-vista-church-hosts-baking-bread-sessions-to-spur-social-change/.

7. Rajendra Pillai, *Reaching the World in Our Own Backyard: A Guide to Building Relationships with People of Other Faiths and Cultures* (Colorado Springs, CO: WaterBrook, 2003) is a helpful resource for cross-cultural interaction, including country-specific guidance.

8. Adapted from Knoxville Internationals Network, "More Than a Book Club" (November 8, 2019), www.kin-connect.org.

9. Jess Berryhill, "More Us, More We," DisAbility Ministry blog (February 22, 2020), https://abilityministry.com/2020/02/22/more-us-more-we-part-3.

10. The Search Institute (search-institute.org) is an excellent source of information about the role of healthy connections for children and youth. America's Kids Belong (faith.americaskidsbelong.org) provides resources for churches interested in helping members of their congregation connect with children and youth as foster families or adoptive "forever" families.

11. "Amachi" is a Nigerian Ibo word meaning "Who knows but what God has brought us through this child."

12. For more on mentoring and other ideas for how churches can build supportive relationships with children, see Ronald J. Sider and Heidi Unruh, eds., *Hope for Children in Poverty: Profiles and Possibilities* (Valley Forge, PA: Judson Press, 2007).

13. For more on trauma informed ministry resources, see chapter 8, and the online resource list. A good training resource specifically for church-based programs is www.belonguniversity.com.

11
Leadership for Connection
Help Your Church Get Organized for
Relational Ministry

If you are a leader in your church, your words, actions, and the way you lead can play an important role in helping your church shift to a focus on real connections. We are defining a leader as any person of responsibility or influence in a congregation, including staff, lay leaders on church boards and committees, people who lead particular programs or ministry areas, and those who lead informally with personal influence.

The first part of this chapter suggests how leaders can model a relational life and incorporate it in their church work. As they carry out their tasks in the church, leaders can develop connections within their team and through their work. In the second part of the chapter, we offer tools for organizing a church-wide effort for a sustained focus on real connections.

Modeling Real Connections

As a leader, your choices regarding real connections can influence other church members. One of the things I (Joy) have paid attention to, about those who have pastored me over the years, is whether they talk about spending time with friends outside the church. Modeling this to church members communicates a vision of a balanced life, not just focused on work and tasks but invested in the lives of others and allowing them to invest in you. Your example can help the people you are leading to keep these ideas in front of them, despite cultural norms of busyness and independence: we all need deeper connections and should make time to develop them.

Sharing authentically about your life and struggles is another key component to being a relational leader. This models for others that it is safe to be real at church. A pastor I (Joy) know recently shared with his congregation the struggles that he has had with his weight over the years and described a new focus on fitness in his life. Over the years, I have witnessed ministry leaders publicly speaking about overcoming addiction, dealing with the grief over the loss of a child, and pursuing mental health care to deal with depression. Admissions such as these serve to show others that it is OK to talk about what is really happening in your life.[1]

The way you handle conflict as a leader will also model for church members that relationships are more important than agreeing on everything or being right. The goal is to keep the value of your relationship with the other person firmly in view, not just seeing them as an obstacle to your goal. Be direct but also kind. We offer tips on handling difficult conversations in chapter 9 of this book.

A picture for me (Joy) in how to handle conflict in church came early in my ministry, when I brought a controversial governance proposal before our church board. One of the elders of our church, whom I respected and considered a friend, argued strongly against what I had proposed. I remember when we went out into the hall after the meeting, he made a point of coming over to me and saying, "I don't agree with your proposal, but I admire your work and we are still friends. What happens in board meetings doesn't affect our friendship."

Leaders can also model being a lifelong learner when it comes to relationships. Build your skill sets for managing relationships such as emotional intelligence and cross-cultural capacities. "Because all ministry has relational roots, even the best skill sets cannot sustain a pastor's ministry [who] doesn't learn to navigate the messiness of relationships."[2] Show the congregation how you are working to grow in listening well, being curious, and the other qualities for making real connections.

Leading with Relationships in Mind

Whatever sort of team you are leading, whether the church board, a committee, or an informal group of volunteers, here are some strategies for keeping relationships a priority, so that team members come away feeling cared for and knowing each other better:

Encourage team members to show care and concern for one another. Start meetings with a personal check-in time when people can share joys and prayer requests with one another. Encourage the group to follow up later on the needs that are expressed. For example, if someone has a child in the hospital, you or another group member can check if the family needs meals or other assistance, then arrange for this to be provided. Even following up with a simple text like "just checking in to see how your daughter is doing today" can make a difference.

Model making time for conversation. Stay connected to group members by making sure to talk with them personally when you see them. Make time for conversations; don't just dash past team members at church. Ask people questions to get them to talk about themselves or about things you know they are interested in. Challenge yourself to continually learn new things about your fellow team members.

Plan time to get to know one another. This can be included in the team's agenda, or the team can talk over a shared meal before the meeting. You can use a lively icebreaker, or establish a standard opener like "What's on your mind today?" Introduce probing questions to get people talking, such as, "Who was your favorite teacher in high school and why?" or "What do you love to do so much you lose track of time?" (See chapter 4 for more ideas for making meetings more relational.) Tools to discover team members' gifts and personality traits can also be illuminating and spark meaningful conversation.

People may balk at first if they are afraid this relational aspect will take over the meeting and prevent other work from getting done. However, if you facilitate the sharing to stay within a set time frame, the interest and energy this generates can make the rest of the agenda go more smoothly. People who know and like one another get more done together.

Use a personal approach to inviting people to join your team. Talk with them about the work of the team, but most importantly, tell them why you think their gifts and skills are especially needed for this work. People aren't cogs to fit into a big ministry machine—show them you see their God-given uniqueness and giftedness when you ask them to help with the task.

Value the person more than performance. Whether offering praise or constructive criticism, share it in a way that reaffirms that you value the team member for who they are, not just what they get done. Make it mutual by inviting their perspective on your leadership. Be sensitive to how other areas of their life might be affecting their involvement.

Create a welcoming atmosphere in meetings. Show team members they matter by setting up the meeting space to encourage interaction, paying attention to their comfort, and maintaining a safe environment in team discussions for open sharing. This affirms to the group, "No matter how humble, how proud or how annoying, you are worthy of respect, love, honor and good-quality coffee."[3]

Getting Planning Work Done with a Focus on People

Making plans and implementing them is a key part of what church leaders do—whether planning for a three-year building project, a summer youth outreach program, or next week's church council agenda. How can your church integrate a focus on connections into this important work?

The answer is to keep the focus on people—recognizing their gifts, gathering their ideas and perspectives, and connecting them with one another. Pay attention to how the planned project may impact relationships. Engaging with people throughout the process may try the patience of those who want to "get on with it," but in the end it strengthens connections and leads to better results.

A connection-centered planning process addresses five questions:

- Whose input needs to be gathered in planning?
- Who could be included in decision making and leading?

- Who has assets we can build on to implement the initiative?
- What goals for relationship are in our desired outcomes?
- Whose feedback will be helpful to improve our efforts?

These elements of a relationally focused planning process are intended to complement, not replace other organizational tasks (like budgeting). They also go hand in hand with praying for discernment and listening to the guidance of the Holy Spirit.

Whose input needs to be gathered in planning? Starting out with lots of listening, rather than a pre-set agenda, is key to a more relational way of planning.[4] Be intentional about seeking input from the groups of people who will be affected by the plan, whether in the church or in the community. Also reach out to people or agencies with expertise in the area of the planned church activity. It can also be helpful to anticipate who might resist the plan, and talk with them. Listen for people's ideas and preferences, what they need and want (and don't want), their relevant previous experiences (good or bad), and their thoughts on how to create opportunities for connections.

The listening process may be informal; for example, when my (Heidi's) husband is preparing a sermon, he will often work his sermon topic into conversations with various folks and then ask, "So what do you think I should say about that?" For planning bigger projects, more formal listening tools can be useful, such as surveys, interviews, and focus groups. See the online listening guides, and see also Joy's book, *Seven Creative Models for Community Ministry* (Valley Forge, PA: Judson Press, 2013), which includes detailed steps to conducting listening processes in the congregation and community.

Who could be included in decision making and leading? Your listening may point to people who have a real passion for this new initiative you are planning. You may want to build a deeper relationship with these folks and tap into their energy in forming a leadership or advisory team for the initiative. Also reach out to people who may not see themselves as leaders, but have an important perspective based on their life experiences. For example, if the church wants to start a budgeting class, consult with people who have faced financial struggles and learned from them. This will expand your circle of connections.

Who has assets we can build on to implement the initiative? Look for people in the congregation and community who can contribute gifts, skills, and other resources. Check also to see who may be doing similar work. For example, if your church would like to offer art classes to youth, connect with the art teacher in your congregation, as well as the youth center and arts organizations in the community.

What goals for relationship are in our desired outcomes? Along with other program goals, identify outcomes that are linked to real connections.[5] This might include:

• Participants now know people that they hadn't gotten to know before.
• Participants spend more time interacting meaningfully with one another.
• Participants have a better appreciation for the importance of making connections.
• Program leaders and volunteers have grown in their caring connections with one another.

Consider how the program might encourage bridging connections (bringing people together across differences) as well as bonding connections (helping people strengthen and deepen their relationships).

First Christian Church in Newburgh, Indiana, experimented with several ways of keeping relational goals in the driver's seat for their community ministry programs, including: talking about relationships when starting a new ministry; having a regular agenda item about relationships in team meetings; and including metrics about relationships in project reports. The team also appointed a member to serve as their "relationship conscience," to provide feedback to the team on the health of their connections—with people in the community, within the team, and with others in the congregation. Larry Groves, an elder at First Christian, offers this advice: "Be ruthless in keeping relationship outcomes as part of the

Connection-Centered Planning Process: Case Study

Imagine that a church wants to start a second worship service geared toward young adults. How could a church integrate a focus on relationships into the process of planning and launching this service?

Input. You talk with many young adults, including some who are not part of the church, about the desire and options for a new service. You listen to the concerns and ideas of church staff who will be involved with the service. And you connect with another church that already offers a service designed for young adults, to ask for their insights.

Decision making. You form a vision team for the new service, with a mix of young adults from the congregation and the community. This team gives input on specific decisions as they arise, such as whether to have a nursery, and what styles of music to include. Their energy and sense of ownership are contagious.

Assets. The vision team recommends adding healthy food to the post-service coffee time instead of the usual donuts. One young adult in the church knows the owners of a health food co-op. After talking with them, they are excited to supply the food needed—and they said they might even come visit the service.

Goals. The team decides to focus initially on two relational outcomes for the service: participating young adults will get to know at least three other attenders by name, and attenders will start hanging out with one another more outside the service. Toward these goals, they decide to nudge service attenders to connect by starting a mid-week coffee club.

Feedback. After four months of the new worship service, the vision team messages all the attenders to ask for their thoughts on how things are going. The vision team meets with the worship leaders for a lunch while sharing observations. They reflect on the question, "What could we do to help the attenders get to know one another better?" Everyone agrees to have a personal talk with one young adult, to see what might help them get more connected.

discussion. You must fight the natural gravity of focus on delivery service as you are making plans."

Whose feedback will be helpful to improve our efforts? Once the plan goes into action, be intentional about getting periodic input from leaders, volunteers, and other participants (inside and outside the congregation) about how things are going. Even if people have negative things to say, they may end up feeling more connected with the church because they were asked for their opinion. You may even find new partners and volunteers because you reached out.

Follow up on this feedback by adapting parts of the plan that looked good on the drawing board but didn't work out for people in real life. Feedback may suggest a need to do more listening and build connections with diverse groups in the church or community. It might even mean deciding to pause current plans if you discover deep divides or overriding needs. The relationships are more important than the program.

Organizing a Connections Leadership Team

In this section, we look at leadership for the broader effort of moving relationships to the center of church life. The natural follow-up question is: Who is going to do the work? We do not recommend putting everything on the pastor. Instead, we recommend that making the shift toward connections be the work of a team (in coordination with the pastor).

There are a few different ways that this work could be organized, depending on your church's structure and circumstances. The simplest option is to utilize an existing leadership group, such as your church's elder board or council, to guide the overall vision and process. This leadership group could then work with the committees or ministry teams responsible for the areas where you would like to make relational shifts (youth, worship, community outreach). Learning together and planning with your current leaders will help strategies for real connections take root in existing ministry areas.

Another option is to form a new short-term team focused on taking steps toward real connections. This is an advantage if current leadership groups are overworked or if the church wants to try innovative programming. Having a separate group also has the advantage of bringing together new people with a different set of perspectives and skills than the "usual suspects" who often populate boards and committees.

This short-term connections team might work for four to six months on the following tasks:

- Explore the current status of relationships in the church.
- Lead processes of listening and asset discovery in the congregation and community (the online resources for this book include a detailed listening guide).
- Research other churches and ministry models that are effectively promoting real connections (see chapter 10).
- Design short-term experiments that the church can try—maybe a new series of get-to-know-you events, or encouraging members to meet

Who to Include on a Connection Team
If you decide to form a connection team, consider a mix that includes representation from:

- church leadership board/council
- staff or lay leaders in areas of church life where connections most likely take place: hospitality, congregational care, small groups, welcoming visitors, community outreach, service
- both long-time and newer members (very different perspectives on church life)
- major demographic groups in the congregation (including youth)
- someone working in a relationally-oriented field (e.g., social worker, community organizer, camp counselor, recreation director)
- someone who lives or works in the neighborhood around the church
- a networker (knows everyone, connects the dots between church and community)
- an empathetic listener who can help nurture relationships in the team

three new neighbors, for example. Chapters 4 to 7 are filled with ideas for you.

• Recommend tweaks to existing programs and ways of doing things that could facilitate connections (such as starting Bible study with a time of checking in with one another).

• Recommend new ministry programs and other long-term initiatives.

Consider a longer-term team (several years, or permanent) if shifting toward connections will be a major focus for your church, with the goal of sustaining changes. The long-term team can be helpful if you plan to launch new initiatives, such as a youth mentoring program or a weekly congregational meal. Having a group to guide sustained effort is also important if you intend to build connections in contexts of high need, entrenched injustice, or social conflict.

Organizational Questions for New Relational Ministry Programs

Use the connection-centered planning process described on pages 132–136 to help in making key organizational decisions for new initiatives with a relational focus.

Scale. Will this be a small-scale experiment or a larger program?

Volunteers. How many and what sort of volunteers will be needed? How will they be recruited and managed?

Finances. Will the new relational activities cost money, and if so, how much? Will the funding be a line item in the church budget or come from somewhere else?

Governance. What steps or groups are involved in obtaining approval for new ideas to move forward? Will the new plan be led by an existing group, or will it require a new leadership structure?

Outcomes. How do you expect people's lives will change because they are able to make real connections through this program? How will progress toward this goal be measured?

The role of a longer-term group could include the tasks of the short-term team listed above, plus:

- Keep relationships as a primary focus for the church.
- Equip and recruit church leaders for a more relational role.
- Help lead significant transitions in how the church does things while paying attention to relationships in this process.
- Oversee the listening process for planning new initiatives and seek feedback as it goes on.
- Communicate these priorities and changes to the congregation.

A clear communications strategy is important to the success of new initiatives. Here are a few key messages the connections team may want to communicate as you are moving along with a listening-based planning process:

- Here's why listening and building relationships is important.
- We are conducting a listening process—would you like to participate?
- Here is what we have learned through our listening process (summarize key findings).
- This is what our new ministry looks like (key activities and calendar).
- We need volunteers/donations for a new ministry—here's how you can help!
- Here's what we're doing differently in order to encourage connections.

Good communication strengthens connection. Frequent updates affirm to people that they are in the loop. If you are engaged in a community listening process, for example, include an update about it in your communication channels every month, even if you've made just a little progress. An effective communication plan adapts to the needs and preferences of various groups (e.g., via emails, texts, printed bulletin, or social media) and includes informal networks and word of mouth.

Keeping Real Connections as a Goal

Church leaders may face pressure to push relationships to the side to focus on more easily measured outcomes like attendance and offerings. We encourage you to keep affirming that relationships are a goal in themselves, a core part of God's design for individuals and the church. Relationship-focused leadership thus brings different questions to discussions of the church's vision and purpose.

Rick Rusaw, pastoring in a city and considered "the least religious in America," described his journey toward a more relationship-centered life and leadership:

> Numbers are important. They are certainly one of the useful ways for leaders to measure growth. For many (me included), we stop with butts, bucks, and baptisms. . . . Nearly every morning for the last three years I have asked God, "How can I love you better today than I did yesterday, and how can I love my neighbors better today than I did yesterday?" . . . Those are the two questions by which we measure ministry. But it's been hard work. Those two questions have given rise to more angst, more wrestling, more failure, and more challenge than anything we have ever done. It's also very hard to measure success compared to anything we have done before. Yet those two questions have also brought clarity, joy, and satisfaction beyond what we have experienced in the past.[6]

This is a leadership challenge, to be sure, but one that has the potential to change the lives of all involved.

Notes

1. There are limits to this: Leaders should have good boundaries about what should not be shared publicly—details of marital difficulties, for example. Avoid personal disclosures that violate someone else's privacy or safety.

2. Jennifer M. Kvamme, "Your Relational Abilities Matter More Than Your Preaching," *EFCA Today* (Winter 2016).

3. Gretchen Ziegenhals, "We Are Called to Be Keepers of an Open Tent," *Faith & Leadership* (May 17, 2016).

4. Dave Odom, "Design Comes to Church," *Faith & Leadership* (November 29, 2016).

5. The relational assessment tool in the online resources may help in suggesting relevant outcomes related to real connections.

6. Brian Mavis and Rick Rusaw, *The Neighboring Church: Getting Better at What Jesus Says Matters Most* (Nashville: Thomas Nelson, 2016), xvii.

12
Navigating Change
Moving Relationships to the Center of Church Life

For many churches, moving relationships to the center will require significant changes. And if a church focuses on relationships, it is likely to be transformed in ways that cannot be anticipated. This chapter is about helping your church manage the shifts that lead to, and come from, real connections.

Change can be hard for churches. We think church is more personal than other kinds of organizations, because it is tied to our personal spiritual beliefs and devotional lives. Also, members' involvement with their church

What Could Change?
Changes you might expect in your church as a result of moving relationships toward the center:

- new kinds of people participating more fully in church life
- more diverse input into planning, leading to different priorities
- slowing the churn of church activities—more time for conversation, less on the calendar
- church routines and programming changed to foster connections
- willingness to use resources on experiments to encourage connections that might or might not work
- support for members pursuing connections in their neighborhoods
- shifts to more relational community ministry as a result of listening and collaboration
- gaining new perspectives on a range of issues as a result of new relationships and deeper sharing of experiences
- greater ability to discuss tough theological and social questions

may be long term and linked with significant events in the life of their family. Church members get used to the way things are, get attached to certain aspects of church life, and may get upset when things change, even in what may seem like minor ways.

Yet our churches *must* change because the world is constantly changing around us. New generations bring both challenges and gifts to the mix. New technology, a more diverse society, and economic and environmental shifts require the church to respond in order to remain both relevant and vital. We believe that congregations centered on relationships are better equipped to adapt. As a church encourages real connections, life-giving innovation will be more likely to spring forth.

So, what can you do to help move your church forward?

Signs of Progress in Moving Toward Real Connections

Start by exploring a vision of what church looks like when relationships come first. If church members are taking the relational focus to heart, what would you expect to see happening? Watch for these signs of progress.

Ministries create time and space for participants to get to know one another better. For example, in addition to teaching about the Scriptures, Bible studies are a place where people learning about one another and helping one another integrate biblical wisdom into their daily lives. Church committees and boards devote time at meetings for discovering one another's gifts and praying for one another.

The congregation tries to make sure no one feels ignored or dispensable. Regular members are attentive to anyone who is sitting alone in church or staying on the edges of church life. Visitors to the church are warmly welcomed and fairly quickly provided with ways to engage with other attenders. Invitations to connection come naturally—one church family inviting a new family over to lunch, for example.

The church engages with people who live and work in the community, having regular conversations with residents and participating in groups that meet about community issues and projects. Ministry programs focused on the community have a more relational focus that is expressed by personally interacting with people served by church programs and recognizing their gifts as well as needs. Church members are volunteering in ways that bring them together with community residents, working side by side as they have opportunities to get to know one another.

Members reach out and build connections as an expression of their faith. Church members are becoming great listeners who look beyond their usual circle to connect with people who may be isolated or in need of a friend. This may be inviting a single-parent family in your neighborhood to a play date at the park, checking in on a homebound elderly church member, mentoring a youth in foster care, or reaching out to befriend someone at work who is grieving a loss.

The church cultivates collaborative relationships. Beyond sharing volunteers, funds or facilities, the church has a personal investment in its partnerships. This could mean getting together with another congregation for regular fellowship meals; providing hospitality for a community group that uses the building; or being a trusted partner with a neighborhood school.

Members are crossing divides through constructive conversations. The church guides members in taking the risk to have difficult conversations, pursue cross-cultural interactions, and build trust with people who have experienced trauma.

Church leadership actively models putting connections first by making room for relationships in their own lives and in the groups they lead. Leaders encourage ideas for new connection-oriented activities as well as ways of making current ministries more relational. Leaders take a structured approach to planning for connections, while remaining open to the fact that relational-focused ministry is often messy and requires reliance on the direction of the Holy Spirit.

We hope this picture is not overwhelming but enticing. We encourage moving forward in small, meaningful steps, knowing that change starts small and grows. You can begin by working on one or two areas, trusting that progress there will help to energize progress in other areas. Which one or two areas in the list above might be a good starting place?

The rest of this chapter will look at the process that fuels progress in these small steps toward change.

Take a Close Look at Your Church's Culture

I (Heidi) formerly attended a church in an area that had a high rate of homelessness and mental health needs. From time to time, someone from the community might enter the church and wander into the sanctuary in the middle of a worship service. Just as often someone might get up suddenly during a service and leave. The regular attenders didn't mind when this happened; they were used to it. Being a welcoming space for all people was part of the church's culture.

Understanding church culture is vital to the goal of moving connections to the center of church life. Since it lies underneath everything else, culture influences what happens at your church without anyone really noticing it or thinking about it. Tod Bolsinger, in *Canoeing the Mountains*, describes how culture is linked with what the church makes most important: "Culture is not the aspired values printed on a poster or put up on a website. Culture is the combination of actual values and concrete actions that shape the warp and woof of organizational life."[1]

A popular saying is "Culture eats strategy for breakfast," meaning, in this case, that if you lay some new program ideas on top of a church culture that is not amenable to new people or to relational ways of doing ministry, not much will change. Therefore, we recommend considering your church's culture before jumping into strategies and activities to develop connections. For example, one church we trained in an asset exercise recognized that it had a very laid-back culture. This did not appear to be an asset as they explored a school partnership; but it was a strength when they started building informal connections with refugee families.

This is why efforts to move in the direction of real connections should work with the church's culture, not against it. Identifying compatible values in your church's culture can help you build connections-focused ministry on what you already do naturally, as well as anticipate the possible barriers. The table below provides examples.

Our church values …	How this value supports relationships	How this value might be a barrier to connections
Families	Lots of kid-friendly activities that connect families for fun and support	People who are single, childless, or in non-traditional households may feel excluded
Stewardship	Great facilities for hosting events that bring people together	Reluctance to let community groups use the facilities for fear they might cause damage
Stability	A solid base of resources for adding activities to build connection	Reticence to add expenses to the budget for anything new
Friendliness	A warm welcome for new people	Prefer shallow connections to authenticity that might expose disunity or conflict
Self-sufficiency	A can-do attitude about using the gifts in the congregation to launch new ventures	Avoid partnerships because it's better to do everything independently
Belonging	Close-knit bonds of mutual care and accountability in the congregation	Sense of belonging only extends to people who are like "us"
Growing	Continually reaching out to connect with new people	Emphasize numerical growth at the expense of deeper relationships

What Values Shape Your Church?
To discover the values that drive your church and its approach to relationships, here are a few fill-in-the-blank questions:

- According to how our church defines "success," we know we are on track when we _____
- Church members would get upset if we changed or stopped _____
- We'd ideally like to be described by others as _____
- We are most willing to spend time and resources on _____

Please note that we are not calling for churches to throw away their culture and values. Rather, we encourage you to consider how to express these foundational elements of church life in a way that supports rather than discourages real connections. Change is more sustainable when you can build on what is already important to you. How can you channel your strengths into a culture of connection?

Prioritizing Relationships and "Getting Work Done"

If your church has a task-oriented culture, leaders may face a tendency to compartmentalize "being relational" from "getting stuff done." It might be assumed that a focus on connections is good for coffee hour and small groups but inefficient when there are important tasks to accomplish.

The first step is to realize that *relational* and *organized* are not opposites. Being focused on relationships is not synonymous with being disorganized, chatty, touchy-feely, or all about warm fuzzies. You don't have to choose between building connections and pursuing excellence in important tasks, like planning an outstanding worship experience or managing an effective community food ministry. A relational focus does, however, mean including connections in the definition of what is considered excellence. It means having the goal that after the tasks get done, the people who did the work will know, support, and trust one another, and those in the community with whom they interact, more than when they started.

A related shift is to redefine what it means to "get stuff done." Some may perceive that relational time is just sitting around and talking and a distraction from getting to the real work. But our premise is that cultivating relationships *is* part of the real work of the church. This can be underscored by including goals related to relationships in planning and evaluating church activities (see chapter 11). Management studies show that the more people know, trust, and empathize with one another, the more effectively they work together.[2] There is a direct correlation between strengthening the quality of relationships and achieving quality outcomes.

Another shift is in realizing that effectiveness in ministry does not necessarily mean "predictable" or "being in control." Relationships are, by their nature, not predictable. You may need to develop a greater degree of comfort with relying less on routines and more on relationships, including leaning on God's Spirit. The upside to this is that when routines get turned upside down—as they did in 2020—your church will already have processes in place to adapt to rapid change and be resilient, based on your focus on connections.

Church Assets That Can Encourage the Shift Toward Relationships

We have described the importance of asset-based thinking throughout the book. As you look at shifting your church toward helping people make real connections, consider the assets and strengths that you already have that will help you to accomplish this (see the asset discovery tool in the online resources). What might first come to mind are your church's physical assets—a kitchen and fellowship hall for making meals and eating together, or a playground for activities with parents and kids. But your church's intangible assets are just as important.

Here is a partial list of assets that can help you move forward.

A tradition of small groups. Having a stock of trained and committed group leaders, and a habit of setting aside time to meet together, provides a natural vehicle for relationships. With intentional effort, small groups can be places where members form lasting bonds—providing mutual support, exploring deep spiritual questions and tough topics, sharing life together.

A tradition of gathering for activities. If your congregation is always getting together to party, do projects, or share meals, you already have a key piece for building connections. Make sure that events are designed to help people to mingle with people they don't know well, or to have deeper conversations with folks they do already know. Otherwise people tend to gravitate toward small talk with friends.

An easy way for people to engage as lay volunteers and leaders. Church members often make deeper connections by working side by side together on a ministry. Inviting people to contribute their time and talents to something meaningful is also a good pathway for engaging with less-connected attenders as well as residents in the community.

People with the gifts of hospitality and encouragement. Some people are extraordinarily gifted at welcoming people, affirming them, and creating environments of hospitality. If you have people like this in your church, value them and let them loose.

People who know how to have fun. Every church has them—high-energy people who lighten every situation with a smile or a joke, and make it easier for people to meet others. They are the ones to consult about how to turn dull meetings into joyful social occasions.

People with entrepreneurial, creative skills. You need people who can imagine a different future, one in which people are more richly connected, and who have creative talents to communicate that vision. You need people who are used to tackling big problems like social isolation, and taking risks to bring new solutions into reality. Artists and entrepreneurs working together can develop new avenues for bringing people together.

Current involvement in the community. If your church is already involved in providing services in the community, that can be a springboard for developing more mutual relationships. Partnerships can help you meet more community residents and have conversations with them.

People with challenging life experiences. People who have gotten through difficult times with the help of supportive relationships are also often the ones who model empathy for others. These folks may be champions for your church's caring connections.

Reliance on one another. Congregations without a lot of funds or technology resources often have the gift of leaning on one another, while leaning together on God. Perhaps your church already has learned to value people above all other assets—and that is at the core of putting relationships first.

Strategies to Support a Shift Toward Relationships

We have acknowledged that change in church is hard—but it is possible. Here are a few strategies that can help as you make progress in moving relationships to the center of church life.

Talk about relationships. If you want your church to become more relational, then talk about that all the time—make it a focus of preaching and teaching, Bible studies and book clubs. Highlight stories about real connections in church newsletters and other regular communication vehicles.

Train people for relationships. Help the congregation understand why relationships are vital and how to take steps toward real connections. Provide short, accessible trainings on how to be a great listener, how to talk with strangers, how to connect with neighbors, how to have safe boundaries. Prepare members to engage warmly with people who are new or loosely connected. Point members to opportunities for more in-depth training in trauma-informed ministry, mental health, cross-cultural interaction, racial justice, and other areas relevant to building restorative relationships.

Include relational goals in ministry planning. Every time you get together to plan, talk about what it looks like to encourage deeper connections in the ministry of your church.[3] Any time there is a report on the status of the church, include reflections on the goal of putting relationships at the center.

"Right-size" your programs and activities. It takes time and energy to build real connections with others. If your church's staff and volunteers

are already maxed out with a busy church calendar, they won't have anything left over to dedicate to the goal of being more relational. You can't do everything, so you may need to sift out activities that impede growth in relationships. If you plan new programs, take care not to add to the busyness of existing leaders and risk burnout.

Keep listening. Any time you intend to try out new ways of connecting, listen to the people in your congregation to gather their best ideas and concerns. When you want to partner or create new programming with the community, listen to residents and leaders to make sure you understand their perspective and come alongside what people are already doing.

Create a process for inclusive innovation. Hold roundtable "blue-sky" dialogues on how to encourage relationship building. Churches can generate a bigger pool of possible ideas when they have all kinds of gifts at the table—teaching, mercy, leadership, administration, prophetic insights, social work, real estate development, and on and on. This lovely mishmash will take shape only if there is an intentional effort to invite everyone into the conversation, and if people around the table are given the chance to discover one another's strengths and vision.

Try small experiments. Chances are good that you will have to try a few approaches before you land on something that works. We recommend you experiment with new approaches—try out small pilots, get feedback and evaluate, then make adjustments and try again (or start over with a different approach).

Give yourself permission to fail. If your congregation has a culture of perfectionism, it will be more difficult to take on new kinds of relational ministry. Relationships will always be messy, unpredictable, and imperfect. Revise your expectations, and educate the congregation so people don't get discouraged when plans don't work as intended. Stay focused on the goal of developing relationships, even if you have to change trains several times along the way.

Be kind. Have we mentioned yet that relationships are messy? Whenever people connect, there is the possibility of hard words and hurt feelings. Develop a culture of showing grace, practicing forgiveness, and being curious instead of critical. (This includes being kind to your-self—if and when you mess up.) This goes a long way in preparing the congregation for new relationships that teach us the meaning of sacrificial love, as Christ has loved us.

Anticipate Resistance

How to deal with opposition to making a shift toward relationships?

Almost every congregation we've worked with has that individual who objects to any change because "that's not the way we've done things"— and there's not much you can do about that. Other sources of resistance specific to a shift to a relational orientation may come from:

- leaders of existing programs that have not been focused on relationships
- budget hawks who don't want to spend money on new activities
- long-time members concerned that bringing in new people or partner-ships might shake up church traditions
- those who fear that new relationships will divert attention from the needs of existing members

One of the best ways to address opposition to relational ministry is by making a real connection. A good starting place is to sit down with naysayers to listen to their concerns. They may have questions or misun-derstandings you can address. Or your new idea may be bringing up painful past experiences. They may also raise valid issues that you hadn't thought about before. Often people don't want to be troublemakers; they just want to be heard. In this process you may get to know them better.

While expanding connections, it's important to take care of existing re-lationships in the congregation. For example, if you've left someone out of the loop who should have been consulted earlier, and now they are of-fended . . . consider apologizing for this oversight. Let them know that their feedback is valued. If a ministry leader feels threatened by the atten-tion given to new programs, perhaps consider publicly expressing appre-ciation for their service.

The biggest barrier you will probably face is fear: fear of scarcity, failure, different-ness, danger, loss. New is scary. New means not being in control. Let's be honest, there are some new people that some church members wouldn't feel comfortable hanging around. There are some connections that don't seem worth the cost. Discerning the difference between legitimate concerns, and fear of the unknown just because it is unknown, can be very hard.

We can offer no easy fixes to the problem of fear. Here's what we do know: as Christians, the way we deal with fear is through relationships. "There is no fear in love, but perfect love casts out fear" (1 John 4:18). Once you start down the path of real relationships, you can be sure that there will be surprises, and that you will be transformed in ways you can't predict. The antidote to fear is openness to the new thing God is doing as we rely on our relationships with God and with one another. Keep taking one small step after another in the direction of real connections.

Making Friends Inch by Inch

The church as an organization can provide the blueprint, the scaffolding, and the resources for building relationships. But only an individual can make a friend. It's up to each of us to walk up to greet a new person, make time for a lunch, have that hard conversation, show up when needed.

Part of making the shift toward a relational church culture is supporting individual members as they take steps toward new connections. This could take many forms.

• Provide times for members to share with one another about their experiences and ideas for connection.

• Help members process the questions and insights that new relationships will bring.

• Lift up how Christians are to relate to others.

• Share resources on how to maintain positive connections, especially in difficult circumstances.

• Offer spiritual guidance as relationships enrich and challenge people's understanding of God.

We all may need our church to remind us that each relationship is its own journey, with steps forward and steps back. We may need reassurance that it's OK to start small and go slow, to be afraid and frustrated sometimes, to learn from our mistakes and accept that others will make them too. That's one way we know it's a real connection.

We close with wisdom from James, age six. James was asked about having friends during the pandemic. He talked about reaching out with friendly overtures to a kid across the street but getting repeatedly rebuffed. "He's older than I am," James observed, "so he thinks I'm stupid." But he keeps trying. "I'm working on making him my friend inch by inch."

Asked why he was being so persistent despite the challenges, James shrugged. "I just want to spend time with my friend and have fun."

When it comes down to it, what could be better than that?

Notes

1. Tod Bolsinger, *Canoeing the Mountains* (Downers Grove, IL: InterVarsity Press, 2015), 74.

2. For example, Charles Duhigg, "What Google Learned from Its Quest to Build the Perfect Team," *The New York Times Magazine* (February 25, 2016); David DeSteno, "To Make a Team More Effective, Find Their Commonalities," *Harvard Business Review* (December 12, 2016).

3. See the tool to assess growth toward relational outcomes in the online resources. See also the set of relational metrics for church leaders in Michael Mather, *Having Nothing, Possessing Everything*, page 127.

Rebuilding Post-Pandemic Connections

In the preface we shared how a year of pandemic distancing reinforced our conviction that living connected with others is central to the church's purpose. As churches readjust to in-person worship, it may be easy to return to "normal" patterns—which sometimes means a calendar filled with activities that may or may not be conducive to building relationships.

How can a commitment to relationships shape how a church helps the congregation and community recover from the pandemic's devastating experiences? What might this look like?

One thing congregations can do is create space for people to process their experiences and grieve together.[1] We can't pretend that everything will be just as it was. Everyone has been touched by the pandemic in some way. Some have suffered the greatest loss—the death of a loved one. Others have lost jobs, school experiences, or holiday family gatherings. We have also all been affected by the social unrest and political upheaval in different ways. People have also witnessed amazing demonstrations of God's faithfulness through it all. We need to talk about it!

Churches can facilitate times of group sharing and prayer that create a sense of solidarity. What has the congregation lost, what roads have been closed, and what new possibilities and opportunities lay before the church? Dialogues may take place in existing groups, such as Sunday school classes or the church leadership council. Churches may also want to organize dialogue groups among people who have been specially impacted, such as health care workers, teachers, and college students. What do people need to be renewed?

A related idea is to organize reconnection conversations, perhaps before or after worship services. This means setting up space, physical or virtual, for people to meet together in pairs or small clusters. Provide starter questions to open up discussion about their experiences, their feelings about the church, their fears and hopes for the country, their dreams for ministry to help restore the community, and their reflections on how they have connected with God through it all.

Another church strategy is to equip a team of listeners, people who are intentional about sitting down with an individual or family in the congregation to ask about their experiences in this turbulent season. These listeners' main role is to pose questions and create a supportive space for people to talk, perhaps offering prayer and a word of encouragement.

In all these connection strategies, be sure to include options for engaging with people who prefer to connect with the church online.[2] Technology for doing life remotely has influenced the way that we cultivate relationships—and we need to talk about that together too.

Churches can also adapt these strategies to connect with the community around issues of post-pandemic restoration. A church can engage in a listening process focused on encouraging people in the community to share their experiences. Working with its community partners, a church can facilitate a time of dialogue within a particular group or in a specific neighborhood. This can take the form of coffee-house-style informal sharing, or a more facilitated process such as World Café.[3] This dialogue can also help community groups develop ideas for going forward with connections, especially among those most vulnerable or isolated.

Setting aside time to interact and process together signals a change in the church's culture, shifting toward meaningful connections as a focal point. Whatever connection activity you do, encourage people to follow up on their own with caring actions and ongoing conversation, whether in person or online. This post-pandemic sharing should not be a one-time event but can lead to a habit of regular listening in the congregation and community (see the listening guides in the online resources). Keep saying to people, "We're in this together."

Notes

1. One resource for this is "Lament Toolkit: Understanding and Practicing Biblical Lament," www.faithward.org/lament-toolkit-understanding-and-practicing-biblical-lament.

2. See resources for dialogue in groups or pairs offered by Essential Partners, www.whatisessential.org/resources.

3. The World Café method brings large groups together for dialogue, with facilitated discussions in groups of four or five people at a table. See Juanita Brown and David Isaacs, *The World Café Book: Shaping Our Futures through Conversations That Matter* (San Francisco: Berrett-Koehler, 2005), www.theworld cafe.com.

1

Safety and Boundaries for Relationships

Any relationship carries some risk, but exercising good judgment and following safety guidelines can prevent many problems.

General Safety Guidelines for Connections

Keep private information private. Until trust is established, take care in sharing your address, phone number, children's names and phone numbers, details of your finances, and whether you live alone.

Avoid potentially risky situations. Before heading into an unknown situation, inform someone you trust where you are going. Don't get into a vehicle with a stranger. Don't be alone with a stranger in a vehicle, home or other private space. Prefer to meet in a public area. If meeting in a room, keep a door open. Having one-one-one meetings in private spaces not only increases the risk that someone might hurt you—it increases the risk that someone might accuse you of hurting them.

Pair up. When doing community listening in residential areas, if you are going door to door talking with folks, it's best not to go alone.

Know when to get help. If you encounter someone dealing with a major trauna such as suicidal thoughts, domestic violence, sexual abuse, trafficking, drug addiction, or a mental health crisis, don't try to handle it on your own. Connect this person with professional assistance. If you lead a relational ministry, make sure your team has contact information for mental health, domestic violence, and substance abuse hotlines.

Safety Guidelines Involving Connections with Children and Youth

If you are involved with a relational ministry program for children and youth, make sure clear safety practices for staff and volunteers are in place. Common guidelines include but are not limited to:

• Never be alone with a child or youth unless it is in a public space.

• Don't accompany children into a bedroom or bathroom (except as needed to assist toddlers).

• Never invite children to your home or take them places without a guardian's permission.

• Don't post pictures of children on your social media without their own and a guardian's consent.

• Be aware of policies in your state regarding mandatory reporting of child abuse and neglect (see www.childwelfare.gov/pubPDFs /manda.pdf).

Volunteers working with children should go through training in safe ministry practices and background checks. Check with your denomination about their policies and resources for safety training (for example, see www.umcdiscipleship.org/equipping-leaders/safe-sanctuaries or www.abusepreventionsystems.com).

Personal Boundaries

Along with general safety guidelines, personal boundaries communicate specifically what is and is not OK with you. This helps you and others stay safe, prevents burnout, and averts conflict.

Personal boundaries can change from person to person and cover a range of areas such as time, money, and physical interaction. Examples of Heidi's boundaries:

• Side hugs are okay with me, but not front hugs or back rubs.

• I don't want to be addressed as "sweetheart" or other terms of endearment, except by my husband.

• If I get calls or texts after 10 pm, or before 8 am, I probably won't answer them, unless it is a family member.

• I may donate money to people if they need it and I have it to give, but I'm not comfortable with making loans.

In a healthy relationship, personal boundaries are communicated and respected. It's OK to tell someone no, or not now, or "I'm not comfortable with that." Honoring your boundaries is not selfish—rather, it's an indication that you respect yourself and that you are likely to show respect to others as well.

Be sensitive to others' boundaries. It's fine to ask people what they are comfortable with. For example, many people are protective of their personal space (even without a virus to worry about). Unless you know they are OK with touch, just smile and wave, or use an elbow bump, air hug, or air high five.

Setting clear boundaries is particularly important in situations involving people who have experienced trauma related to violations in their past. Boundaries are essential to help create the security needed to build trusting and healthy relationships. See *Neighborology: Practicing Compassion as a Way of Life* by David Apple for more on setting boundaries in the context of caring ministry and dealing with difficult people.

Relational Red Flags

Red flags in relationships are signs that this may be an unsafe or unhealthy connection. Red flags to look for include:

• lack of respect for boundaries that have been communicated
• unwillingness to express any boundaries—going along with what everyone else does
• motivations of guilt or fear ("They'll stop being my friend if I don't . . .")
• blaming, shaming, and other controlling behaviors
• feeling unsafe, anxious, or uncomfortable around the person

• persistent use of hurtful labels, stereotypes, and racist language and attitudes
  • interactions have unwelcome romantic or sexual overtones
  • there is secrecy around the relationship
  • the relationship starts crowding out other friendships and activities

If you become aware of any of these red flags, tell someone whose perspective you trust. Step back from the connection for a while. If you feel a sense of relief and security, that tells you this relationship is probably not healthy and either needs to be repaired or left behind. Saying no to an unsafe connection frees space and energy for other relationships.

Self-Care

"Love your neighbor as you love yourself" (Mark 12:31). When you pay attention to what you need to take care of yourself, physically and emotionally, this directly affects the quality of your relationships with others. It's hard to muster the energy and patience for real connections if you are exhausted, stressed, or unwell.

Sometimes being there for others means sacrificing our own comfort and agenda. Sometimes it is a struggle to balance new connections with important time for family and cherished friends. Over the long haul, however, respecting your own needs and the needs of those closest to you is essential for a relationship-rich life.

2
Questions to Build Connection

Getting to Know You

There are many lists of icebreakers and getting-to-know-you questions to be found online. Here is a sample:

What is your favorite time of day and why?
What's something you do well that makes you happy when you do it?
When life gets to you, what or who picks you up?
What's something people might be surprised to learn about you?
Tell a story about a friend you had as a kid or teen.

Getting to Know You—Deeper

What would you be doing in five years, if it were totally your choice?
What color comes to mind when you think about your childhood?
What's a challenge you've faced that you've made progress on?
What is your first memory of learning about God?
Tell a story about a time someone was really there for you.

Curious Questions—General Invitations to Conversation

What's your favorite . . .
What is/was it like to . . .
Tell me about a time when . . .
What do you think/how do you feel about . . .
What do you like most about . . .
I'd love to hear more about . . .

Quick Meeting Starters

What's on your mind right now?

Where have you seen God at work?

What made you smile today?

When did you see someone being kind?

Quick Meeting Closers

What do you appreciate about the person sitting next to you?

What are you looking forward to?

If your life had a soundtrack, what would be playing you out the door?

Give someone a three-word blessing.

Invite Sharing Life Stories

What is a story you like to tell about your childhood or teen years?

What do you want others to understand about your past and how you got to where you are now?

What is a challenge that you have faced in your life? How have you worked to overcome it?

If someone made a movie of your life, what scenes would be important to you to include?

Who are the people who have been most important to you?

What do you hope your future looks like?

See Life Interview Questions, https://legacyproject.org/guides/lifeintquestions.pdf

Intergenerational Neighborhood Interviews

These questions would be appropriate for kids to use with elders and long-term residents in their neighborhood.

1. How did you come to live in this neighborhood?
2. How has the neighborhood changed over time?
3. What do you like to look at out of your window?

4. What do you like best about living in this neighborhood?

5. What is one thing you'd like to see change in this neighborhood?

6. What is something exciting you remember happening in this neighborhood?

When Someone Needs a Supportive Friend

Do you want to set a time when we can talk?

How would you like me to be supportive? Is there something I can do, or is it better for you if I just listen?

How can I pray for you?

What do you see as your options?

What resources or support could be helpful to you?

To Discover Someone's Assets

Support. What people or organizations do you trust to turn to when you need support, beyond your immediate family?

Skills. What are three things you know how to do well? This could include skills developed through training (e.g., car repair, web design); life experiences (childcare, speaking Spanish); or a hobby (music, crafts)

Qualities. What are three personality strengths or natural abilities you have? (Examples: encouraging, networking, beautifying)

Experience. What is something valuable you have gained through your life experiences? (Examples: an achievement that gives you pride, an influence that shaped you, an obstacle you overcame)

Motivators. What one to three issues or concerns do you care deeply about, that motivate you to act?

People. Which groups of people do you especially identify with or connect well with and want to support? (Examples: preschoolers, business owners, immigrants, single parents)

To Help Someone Make Progress Toward a Goal

Instead of giving advice or telling someone what to do, ask:

What makes this goal important to work on now?

What would progress toward this goal look like?

What do you know from training or experience that can guide you?

What skills, strengths, and resources do you have to help you?

What information or resources are you missing?

What is the next step you can try?

What are some options for dealing with the obstacles in your path?

What are the pros and cons of this approach?

What kind of help or support from others do you need?

What can we celebrate about the progress you've made so far?

To Explore Someone's Perspective

When discussing a belief, issue, or worldview:

What has gone into shaping your perspective on this subject?

How does this subject affect people you care about?

Tell about a time this was especially important to you.

What is one thing about your perspective you wish others understood better?

What about this subject have you found most challenging? Most rewarding?

When It's Hard to Listen

If a conversation gets uncomfortable or painful ask:

What is important to me about this relationship?

What is important to me in this conversation?

What might be different or more complicated than I expected?

What can I learn, or how can I grow, from this person?

What does following Jesus look like in this relationship?

What do I need to take care of myself in this conversation?